The Ultimate British

Ninja

Dual Zone

Air Fryer Cookbook

Easy to Make, and Absolutely Delicious Classic Recipes from Traditional Roasts to Quick Weeknight Meals, Colourful Photos for Every Recipe

Mildred Charlton

No part of this publication may be reproduced, distributed, or transmitted in any form or by any means, including photocopying, recording, scanning or other electronic or mechanical Preparations, without the prior written permission of the publisher. Request to the publisher for permission should be addressed to the permission department.

BALVAIRD PUBLISHING — Balvaird Publishing LLC

Author: Mildred Charlton
Editor: Hanley Knight
Illustrator: Glen Franklin

ISBN 978-1-960797-48-3 (Paperback).
ISBN 978-1-960797-37-7 (eBook).

INTRODUCTION

I'm so excited to share some of my favourite Ninja dual zone recipes with you. Whether you're an experienced or a beginner user, I'm sure you'll find something you love. I've included a variety of recipes, from classic British mains to delicious desserts. With clear instructions, helpful tips, British English terminologies and inspiring photos, and only including ingredients that are available to buy from UK supermarkets, you'll be able to create delicious meals in no time. So, let's get cooking!

Mildred Charlton

NINJA DUAL ZONE 101

MAKE MANY DELICIOUS MEALS WITH EASE.

The Ninja Dual Zone air fryer is an amazing kitchen appliance that can help you make many delicious meals with ease. It can air fry, bake, roast, max crisp and dehydrate. With the Ninja Dual air fryer 2 cooking zones, you can cook different foods at the same time. It's perfect for busy households that don't have a lot of time to prepare meals.

EXPERT GUIDANCE ON HOW TO USE YOUR NINJA DUAL ZONE

In this guide I'll guide you through everything you need to know, including how it works, the best foods to air fry, how to clean it, and other useful hints for making the most of your Ninja Dual Zone air fryer! and will leave you feeling confident to get you started in the kitchen .

>>>>>

USING YOUR Dual Zone FUNCTIONS

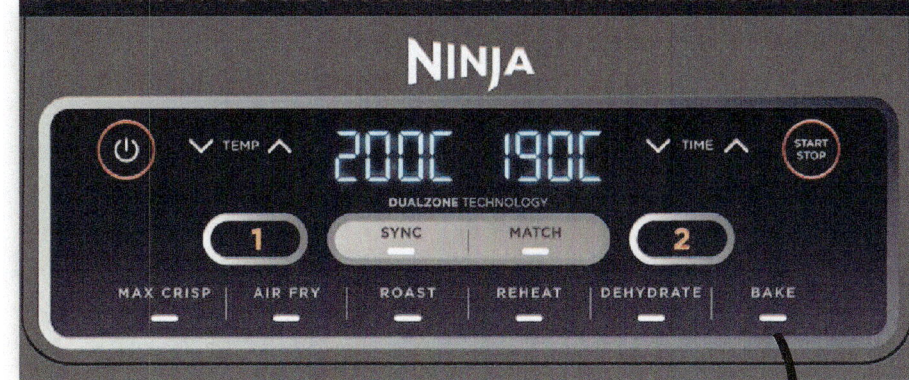

1. The Dual Zone Technology:

You can cook the same food in each zone with the same function, use **MATCH** to automatically duplicate settings In Zone 1 and Zone 2.

You can cook two separate dishes in two different ways (choose from six functions) at the same time, then **SYNC** them to finish at the exact appropriate time so that everything arrives at the table hot.

The Ninja Dual Zone mode includes 6 functions:

- **MAX CRISP :** Ideal for frozen foods such as Chips and Fish fingers.

- **AIR FRY :** Cooks food quickly without drying it out. For guilt-free fried foods that are moist and juicy on the inside while remaining crispy on the outside.

- **ROAST :** Use your Ninja Foodi Dual Zone air fryer as Conventional oven to roast meats.

- **REHEAT :** Warming leftovers gently will bring them back to life, resulting in crispy results.

- **DEHYDRATE :** Dehydrate fruits and vegetables for delicious snacks or dehydrate herbs to reduce food waste.

- **BAKE :** Make fluffy cakes, scones, biscuits and breads at home.

Getting Started

Here are some basic Tips When Using The Ninja Dual Zone Air Frye:

1. *Always place your Ninja Dual Zone Air Fryer* on a flat, heat-resistant surface, and leave at least 13-cm of space behind the air fryer for the exhaust vent.

2. *Don't overcrowd the drawers.* Over-crowding the drawers will prevent foods from crisping and browning evenly and take longer cooking time.

3. *Occasionally shake the ingredients while air frying.* Open the drawers and shake or toss the ingredients for even browning. When finished, reinsert drawers and continue cooking.

4. *Check the doneness of your food as many times as you want.* This is one of the nicest features of the Ninja dual zone air fryers: you can open the drawer at any time during the cooking time to check on the cooking process. The cooking process will resume where it left off when you reinsert the drawers into the air fryer.

5. *Clean the drawer* as well as the crisping plates after every use.

6. *Reduce the temperature by 10°C* when converting recipes from a conventional oven to Ninja Dual Zone Air Fryer and reduce cooking time by 20% . To avoid overcooking, check the food frequently .

⚠️ **NOTICE**

Always refer to your specific Ninja Dual Zone Air Fryer model's manual for detailed instructions and safety precautions.

Cleaning the Ninja Dual Zone Drawers and Crisping Plates:

- Clean the Drawers and the Crisping plates after every use. But let The Unit Cool Down first before you start to clean it.

- The Drawers and the Crisping plates are dishwasher-safe, but hand washing is recommended because it protects the Non-Stick coating.

- If there is a lot of oil and residue on the crisper plate, or drawers, soak them in warm, soapy water.

- If scrubbing is required, use a non-abrasive sponge to avoid scratching or damaging the nonstick coating.

- To clean the outside of your Ninja Dual Zone, Wipe with damp cloth. NEVER immerse the main unit in water or any other liquid.

Best Ninja Dual Zone Air Fryer Accessories:

Tips When Choosing Ninja Dual Zone Air Fryer Accessories:

- Any bakeware marked "oven safe" will work with Ninja Dual Zone air fryers.
- Choose Bakeware or baking dishes with No Handles
- Know your Ninja Dual Zone air fryer drawer's INTERIOR size, not its total capacity.

My Favorite Accessories for Ninja Dual Zone Air Fryer:

1 lb Loaf Tins

Silicone Tongs

Silicone Muffin Cups

Small Tart Tins

While silicone liners can be convenient for cleanup, they don't conduct heat, hinder air circulation, and slow down crisping. Cooking directly on the crisping plate or drawer for best results.

CONTENTS

Introduction 3

Ninja Dual Zone Air Fryer 101 4

Breakfast 9

Starters & Sides 25

Dinners & Suppers 35

Afternoon Tea 85

Index 106

Breakfast

Delicious everyday breakfasts and amazing brunches.

Breakfast

Carmalised Onion and Cheese Quiche

Serves : 6   Prep Time : 20 Mins   Cook Time : 15 Mins

Ingredients

For the crust:
- 200g plain flour
- ½ tsp salt
- 100g cold butter, cut into cubes
- 1 large egg
- Cold water, as needed

Filling:
- 1 large onion, thinly sliced
- 8 tbsp water
- 1 tsp caster sugar
- 150g grated Cheddar
- 4 large eggs
- 100ml milk
- 200ml double cream
- Salt and pepper to taste

Recipe tip:

Pie crust: You can use a store-bought ready rolled shortcrust pastry.

Quiche Variation:

- **Goat Cheese & Roasted Pepper:** Crumble goat cheese, scatter roasted red pepper & sun-dried tomato pieces over the caramelised onions before adding the egg mixture.
- **Spinach and Feta:** add chopped spinach and crumbled feta cheese over the caramelised onions before adding the egg mixture.

Preparation

1. In a bowl, add flour, butter, salt and rub the butter with hands into the flour until resembles breadcrumbs. Add the egg and 1 tbsp water at a time, mix then bring together in a ball (if its too dry add more water, 1 tbsp at a time).

2. On a floured surface roll the dough into 1/2-cm thickness. Grease 6 individual pie tins and line with pie crust. Line the pies with foil and fill with baking beans. Place in zone 1 drawer.

3. With no crisping plate installed, place onion, water, sugar, and pinch of salt in the Zone 1 drawer and stir to combine.

4. Select Zone 1, select BAKE, set temperature to 160°C, and set time to 4 minutes. Select zone 2, select BAKE, set temperature to 160°C and set time to 13 minutes. Select SYNC. Press the START/PAUSE button to begin cooking. (When time reaches 8 minutes, remove drawer from unit and stir. Reinsert drawer to continue cooking).

5. When cooking is complete, transfer onions to a bowl. Then add eggs, milk, cream, cheddar , salt, and pepper. Whisk until combined.

6. Pour the egg mixture into the pie crusts. Place pie tins in zone 1 & 2 drawers (with crisper plate inserted), then insert drawers in unit.

7. Select Zone 1, select BAKE, set temperature to 160°C and set time to 15 minutes. Select MATCH. Press START/STOP to begin.
When the cooking is complete, let set for 5 minutes, then serve.

Carmalised Onion and Cheese Quiche

For your next special breakfast, brunch, lunch, or supper, make this rich, delicious caramelised onion quiche. Made with flavourful Cheddar cheese, it's sure to be a new favourite.

Breakfast

Sausage and Hash Brown Breakfast Casserole

Serves : 2-3   Prep Time : 5 Mins   Cook Time : 25 Mins

Ingredients

- 400g grated potatoes
- 200g broccoli florets
- 4 sausages, cut into bite sized pieces
- 1 tbsp oil
- 5 large eggs
- 2 tbsp milk
- 60g grated cheddar cheese
- 1 red bell pepper, finely chopped
- Salt and pepper to taste

Recipe tip:

Customize the seasoning blend to your taste. You can include herbs like thyme, oregano, paprika or adding a splash of hot sauce, Worcestershire sauce, or mustard for for extra flavour.

Preparation

1. Without a crisping plate inserted, brush zone 1 and 2 drawers with oil.

2. Divide grated potatoes, broccoli and sausage pieces evenly among the two drawers, sprinkle with oil. Insert drawers in unit. Select Zone 1, select AIR FRY, set temperature to 190°C and set time to 12 minutes. Select MATCH. Press START/STOP to begin. (When time reaches 6 minutes, remove drawers from unit and shake drawers. Reinsert drawers to continue cooking).

3. In a bowl add eggs, milk, cheese, bell pepper, salt, and pepper, whisk until combined.

4. When the cooking is complete, pour egg mixture over the potatoes and sausage mixture in Zone 1 and 2 drawers. Insert both drawers into unit.

5. Select Zone 1, select BAKE, set temperature to 170°C and set time to 13 minutes. Select MATCH. Press START/STOP to begin. When the cooking is complete, let set for 5 minutes, then serve.

Breakfast

Potato and Feta Frittata

Serves : 2   Prep Time : 5 Mins   Cook Time : 35 Mins

Ingredients

- 2 medium potatoes, peeled and diced
- 2 tbsp oil
- 1 tsp paprika
- 5 large eggs
- 120g crumbled feta cheese
- 2 tbsp milk
- 2 spring onions, finely chopped
- Salt and pepper to taste

Recipe tip:
Spread the cooked potatoes evenly in the drawer before adding the egg mixture.

Frittata Variation:
Feel free to customise the frittata with additional ingredients like cooked sausage, cooked chicken, crumbled Stilton, mushrooms, spinach or sun-dried tomatoes.

Preparation

1. In a bowl, add the potatoes and oil, mix until all potatoes coated with oil. With crisping plate installed, place the potatoes in zone 1 drawer.

2. Insert drawer in unit. Select Zone 1, select AIR FRY, set temperature to 190°C and set time to 15 minutes. Press START/STOP to begin. (When time reaches 7 minutes, remove drawer from unit and shake drawer. Reinsert drawer to continue cooking).

3. In a bowl add eggs, milk, paprika, salt, and pepper, whisk until combined. Add the spring onions and feta, Stir gently.

4. When cooking is complete, transfer potatoes into a baking dish and pour egg mixture over the potatoes. Place the dish into Zone 1 drawer. Insert drawer into unit.

5. Select Zone 1, select BAKE, set temperature to 160°C and set time to 20 minutes. Press START/STOP to begin. When the cooking is complete, let set for 5 minutes, then serve.

Potato and Feta Frittata

Easy to make and incredibly satisfying, this Potato and Feta Frittata is bursting with flavour and perfect for sharing with family and friends.

Baked Sweet Potatoes

Serves : 2 **Prep Time : 5 Mins** **Cook Time : 40 Mins**

Ingredients

- 2 medium sized sweet potatoes

Preparation

1. Pierce the sweet potatoes all over with a fork. Insert a crisper plate in Zone 1 drawer. Place the sweet potatoes in the drawer.

2. Select Zone 1, select AIR FRY, set temperature to 190°C, and set time to 35-40 minutes. Press the START/PAUSE button to begin cooking. When the cooking is complete, split the sweet potatoes in half open and serve with your favourite toppings. (Such as crumbled Stilton cheese and chopped walnuts or top with a generous dollop of clotted cream and a spoonful of your favourite jam, such as strawberry or raspberry.)

Jacket Potatoes

Serves : 2 **Prep Time : 5 Mins** **Cook Time : 40 Mins**

Ingredients

- 2 (350g each) King Edward or Maris Piper potato
- 1 tbsp oil
- Salt and pepper to taste

Preparation

1. Pierce the potatoes all over with a fork. Rub the potatoes with oil. Season with salt and pepper. Insert a crisper plate in Zone 1 drawer. Place the potatoes in the drawer.

2. Select Zone 1, select AIR FRY, set temperature to 200°C, and set time to 40 minutes. Press the START/PAUSE button to begin cooking. When the cooking is complete, slice open each potato, and serve with desired toppings. (such as thinly sliced roast beef and a dollop of horseradish sauce or top with baked beans and a sprinkle of grated cheese.)
For a Shepherd's Pie-inspired topping: Top with cooked mince. Sprinkle with grated cheese and bake for more 5 minutes until the cheese is melted and bubbly.

Breakfast

Chickpea Baked Eggs

Serves : 4   Prep Time : 10 Mins   Cook Time : 27 Mins

Ingredients

- 1 onion, finely chopped
- 3 tbsp water
- 1 red bell pepper, chopped
- 2 garlic cloves, minced
- 1 tsp smoked paprika
- 1 (400g) tin chopped tomatoes
- 400g tin chickpeas, rinsed and drained
- 4 large eggs
- Salt & pepper to taste

Don't forget the cheese! Before serving, you can either crumble some feta over the top or grate some Parmesan for a proper cheesy finish. It'll add a lovely finishing touch, whatever you choose!

Preparation

1. With no crisping plate installed, place all ingredients (except eggs) in the Zone 1 drawer and stir to combine.

2. Select Zone 1, select BAKE, set temperature to 190°C, and set time to 20 minutes. Press the START/PAUSE button to begin cooking.(When time reaches 10 minutes, remove drawer from unit and stir. Reinsert drawer to continue cooking).

3. When cooking is complete, remove drawers and make 4 wells in tomato mixture. Crack one egg in each well. Season with salt and pepper. Reinsert drawers.

4. Select Zone 1, select BAKE, set temperature to 170°C and set time for 7 minutes. Press the START/PAUSE button to begin cooking. When cooking is complete, remove drawers and serve with crusty bread.

Sausage and Egg Omelette

Serves : 4   Prep Time : 5 Mins   Cook Time : 23 Mins

Ingredients

- 1 medium onion, finely chopped
- 4 sausages, cut into bite size pieces
- 3 tbsp crumbled Stilton
- 6 eggs
- 4 tbsp double cream
- ½ tsp garlic powder
- Salt and pepper to taste
- Optional: peppers, tomatoes or other vegetables of your choice, cut into cubes

Omelette Variation:

Ditch the sausage, add smoked salmon pieces and chopped fresh dill to the egg mixture, follow the rest of the recipe and you'll have yourself a fantastic smoked salmon and dill omelette in no time!

Preparation

1. With no crisping plate installed, place sausage, onion, chopped vegetables (if using) in the Zone 1 and 2 drawers and stir to combine.

2. Select Zone 1, select AIR FRY, set temperature to 200°C, and set time to 10 minutes. Select MATCH. Press the START/PAUSE button to begin cooking. (When time reaches 5 minutes, remove drawers from unit and stir. Reinsert drawers to continue cooking).

3. In a bowl, add eggs, double cream, garlic powder, Stilton, salt and pepper. Whisk until combined.

4. When the cooking is complete, pour egg mixture **over the sausage and vegetables in Zone 1 and 2 drawers. Insert both drawers into unit.**

5. Select Zone 1, select BAKE, set temperature to 160°C and set time to 13 minutes. Select MATCH. Press START/STOP to begin. Stir once after 5 minutes.
When the cooking is complete, let set for 5 minutes, then serve.

Breakfast

Corned Beef Hash

Serves : 2   Prep Time : 5 Mins   Cook Time : 33 Mins

Ingredients

- 600g potatoes, peeled and cut into ½-cm cubes
- 1 onion, finely chopped
- 1 garlic clove, minced
- 340g tin corned beef, finely chopped
- 1 tbsp oil
- 2 eggs
- Salt and pepper to taste

Preparation

1. Toss the potatoes and onion in oil and place the potatoes and onion mixture in zone 1 drawer (With no crisping plate installed), then insert drawer in unit.

2. Select Zone 1, select AIR FRY and set temp to 200°C and set time to 20 min. Press the START/ STOP button to begin cooking. When time reaches 10 minutes, remove drawer from unit and shake drawer for 10 seconds. Reinsert drawer to continue cooking.

3. When cooking is complete, remove drawer. Add the corned beef, stir. Select AIR FRY and set temp to 200°C and set time to 5 min. Press the START/ STOP button to begin cooking.

4. When cooking is complete, remove drawers. Make 2 wells in corned beef hash mixture. Crack an egg into each well. Sprinkle with salt and **pepper**.

5. Place drawer back into unit. Select AIR FRY and temp to 170°C and set time to 8 min. Press the START/ STOP button to begin cooking.

6. Scoop out one egg and the corned beef hash into a plate. Repeat with remaining egg and hash for second serving.

Breakfast

Corned Beef Fritters

Serves : 4   Prep Time : 20 Mins   Cook Time : 10 Mins

Ingredients

- 2 eggs
- 340g tinned corned beef, cut into 1-cm cubes
- 100g self raising flour
- 50g breadcrumbs
- 1 tbsp onion powder
- 3 tbsp oil
- Salt and pepper to taste

Preparation

1. In a large bowl, add the flour, breadcrumbs, onion powder, salt, pepper and mix. Add in eggs and whisk until all combined. Add the corned beef. Stir gently.

2. Use a scoop to add portions of the mixture into a sheet pan and flatten slightly to get an even thickness (make 12 fritters). Place in freezer for 20 minutes.

3. Add the fritters in a single layer in zone 1 & 2 drawers (with crisper plate inserted), brush with oil, then insert drawers in unit. Select zone 1, Select AIR FRY and set temperature to 200°C and time to 10 minutes. Select MATCH. Press the START/ STOP button to begin cooking. Flip halfway through.

4. Sprinkle the fritters with salt if desired and serve.

Breakfast

Cheese and Onion Pasties

Serves : 6   Prep Time : 35 Mins   Cook Time : 30 mins

Ingredients

For the shortcrust pastry:
- 450g plain flour
- 225g cold butter, cut into small cubes
- Pinch of salt
- Cold water
- 1 egg, whisked (for brushing)

For The Filling:
- 2 large onion, thinly sliced
- 4 tbsp water
- 1 tsp dried thyme
- 250g grated mature Cheddar
- 1 tsp English mustard
- 1 tbsp butter
- Salt & pepper to taste

Preparation

1. In a bowl, add flour, salt. Mix. Add butter, and rub with hands into the flour until mixture resembles breadcrumbs. Add water gradually while mixing until a dough comes together (Do Not over mix). Shape into a ball, cover with clingfilm and refrigerate for 30 Minutes.

2. With no crisping plate installed, place onion, water, butter, thyme and pinch of salt in the Zone 1 drawer and stir to combine.

3. Select Zone 1, select BAKE, set temperature to 160°C, and set time to 12 minutes. Press the START/PAUSE button to begin cooking. Stir halfway cooking time.

4. When cooking is complete, transfer onions to a bowl. Then add cheddar, mustard, salt, and pepper. Mix.

5. Divide pastry into 6 balls. Transfer into a floured surface, then roll out each ball into 15-cm circle.

6. Fill each circle with filling mixture on one side and brush edges with egg. Fold half of the pasty over filling and seal the edges. Brush with egg.

7. Insert a crisper plates in both drawers. Place 3 pasties in each drawer, insert drawers in unit. Select Zone 1, select AIR FRY, set temperature to 160°C, and set time to 18 minutes. Select MATCH. Press the START/PAUSE button to begin cooking. (flipping after 10 minutes).

8. When cooking is complete, transfer to a plate. let cool for 5 minutes before serving.

Breakfast

Baked Porridge Cups

Serves : 12 cups Prep Time : 5 Mins Cook Time : 17 Mins

Ingredients

- 350ml milk
- 2 eggs
- 120ml golden syrup
- 60g melted butter
- 120g yogurt
- 80g dried fruits or mixed nuts
- 250g porridge oats
- 1 tsp baking powder
- 1 tsp ground cinnamon
- Pinch of salt

Preparation

1. Grease 12 individual silicone muffin cups.

2. In a bowl, add all ingredients and mix until combined. Spoon porridge mixture evenly into muffin cups. Fill all the way to the top.

3. Insert the crisper plates in zone 1 and 2 drawers. Place muffin cups on crisper plate. Insert drawers in unit.

4. Select Zone 1, select AIR FRY, set temperature to 170°C and set time to 17 minutes. Select MATCH. Press START/STOP to begin.

5. When cooking is complete, remove from unit and cool for 10 minutes before serving.

Porridge Cups Variation:

Sticky Toffee Pudding Inspired: simply chuck in some chopped dates and a good drizzle of toffee sauce (instead of golden syrup) into the porridge mixture to mimic the flavours of the traditional sticky toffee pudding, an absolute winner!

Breakfast

Cheese on Toast

Serves : 2-4   **Prep Time : 2 Mins**   **Cook Time : 7 Mins**

Ingredients

- 4 white bread slices
- Softened butter
- 200g grated cheddar cheese
- Worcestershire sauce

Preparation

1. Butter one side of bread slices with softened butter.

2. Insert the crisper plates in zone 1 and 2 drawers. Place bread slices on crisper plates. Select Zone 1, select AIR FRY, set temperature to 170°C and set time to 2 minutes. Select MATCH. Press START/STOP to begin.

3. When cooking is complete, remove drawers from unit and add cheese on top of each bread slice, press down the cheese onto the bread and add a few drops of Worcestershire sauce on top. Reinsert drawers to unit.

4. Select Zone 1, select BAKE, set temperature to 180°C and set time to 5 minutes. Select MATCH. Press START/STOP to begin.
   When cooking is complete, serve immediately.

Breakfast

Broccoli and Mushroom Omelette

Serves : 4   Prep Time : 3 Mins   Cook Time : 13 Mins

Ingredients

- 6 large eggs
- 1 small tomato, chopped
- 100g frozen broccoli florets, thawed
- 100g button mushroom, sliced
- 60g of your favourite grated cheese
- 6 tbsp milk
- Salt and pepper to taste

Preparation

1. In a bowl, add all ingredients and whisk until combined.

2. With no crisping plate installed, grease Zone 1 and 2 drawers. Then pour egg mixture into both drawers evenly.

3. Select Zone 1, select BAKE, set temperature to 160°C, and set time to 13 minutes. Select MATCH. Press the START/PAUSE button to begin cooking.

4. When cooking is complete, serve.

Breakfast

Celeriac Rosti

Serves : 4 **Prep Time : 10 Mins** **Cook Time : 20 Mins**

Ingredients

- 600g celeriac, peeled and grated
- 2 large eggs
- 1 garlic clove, minced
- 1 small onion, finely chopped
- 5 tbsp plain flour
- Salt and pepper to taste

Recipe tip:
After grating, be sure to squeeze out as much excess moisture as possible from the celeriac/potatoes using a clean kitchen towel.

Rosti Variation:
For Potato Rosti: substitute the grated celeriac with an equal amount of grated potato. You'll end up with a proper crispy potato rosti, enjoy!

Preparation

1. In a large bowl, add all ingredients and mix until combined. Shape into 8 rosits.

2. Insert the crisper plates in zone 1 and 2 drawers. Brush plates with oil. Place 4 rosits on each crisper plate.

3. Select Zone 1, select AIR FRY, set temperature to 180°C and set time to 20 minutes. Select MATCH. Press START/STOP to begin.

4. When time reaches 10 minutes, remove drawers from unit and flip the rostis. Reinsert drawers to continue cooking.

5. When the cooking is complete, use silicone coated tongs to remove the rostis to a serving dish and serve.

Starters & Sides

A selection of delicious starters and sides, that will complete your meals.

Honey Roasted Parsnips

Serves : 4   Prep Time : 5 Mins   Cook Time : 18 Mins

Ingredients

- 500g parsnips, peeled and cut into chips
- 3 tbsp oil
- 1 tbsp wholegrain mustard
- 2 tbsp runny honey
- ½ tsp dried thyme
- Salt and pepper to taste

Recipe tip:

The secret's all in the chop!
Make sure you cut the parsnips/carrots into same size pieces to ensure they'll all be done at the same time, no soggy bits or burnt ends!

Parsnips Variation:

- You can use carrots instead of parsnips, or better yet, use both for a proper colourful roast!
- Just before you serve the parsnips/carrots, give them a good sprinkle of grated Parmesan for a posh finish.

Preparation

1. In a bowl, add parsnips, and oil. Mix until combined.

2. Insert the crisper plates in zone 1 and 2 drawers. Brush plates with oil. Place parsnips on crisper plates. Select Zone 1, select AIR FRY, set temperature to 200°C and set time to 15 minutes. Select MATCH. Press START/STOP to begin. Shaking the drawers every 5 minutes.

3. When cooking is complete, remove drawers from unit and add the honey, mustard, thyme, salt, pepper and shake to fully coat the parsnips. Reinsert drawers to continue cooking.

4. Select Zone 1, select AIR FRY, set temperature to 190°C and set time to 3 minutes. Select MATCH. Press START/STOP to begin.
When cooking is complete, serve immediately.

Starters & Sides

Breaded Baked Aubergine

Serves : 4   Prep Time : 5 Mins   Cook Time : 11 Mins

Ingredients

- 1 large aubergine
- 1 tbsp oil
- 5 tbsp plain flour
- 1 egg
- 120g breadcrumbs
- 50g grated Parmesan
- 1 tsp dried oregano
- 1 tsp dried basil
- ½ tsp dried thyme
- Salt and pepper to taste

Aubergine Variation:

Let's turn it into a cracking Aubergine Parmesan. once they're cooked, give those aubergine slices a good brush with marinara sauce or passata , a sprinkle of Parmesan and a generous amount of grated mozzarella. Pop it back into the ninja and AIR FRY at 190°C for 2 minutes until that cheese is melted.

Preparation

1. Cut the aubergine into rounds 2-cm thick. Place the aubergine slices on a paper towel-lined baking sheet and sprinkle both sides with salt. Let them sit for about 15 minutes to release excess moisture.

2. Rinse the aubergine and pat each slice dry with paper towels.

3. In a shallow bowl, add flour, in another bowl, add the egg and whisk. In a third bowl, add breadcrumbs, thyme, basil, oregano and Parmesan. Mix.

4. Coat each aubergine slice in flour, then dip into the egg. Coat the slices in the breadcrumb mixture, pressing gently.

5. Insert the crisper plates in zone 1 and 2 drawers. Brush plates with oil. Place aubergine slices on crisper plates. Sprinkle with oil. Select Zone 1, select AIR FRY, set temperature to 190°C and set time to 11 minutes. Select MATCH. Press START/STOP to begin. When time reaches 5 mins, remove drawer, flip the aubergine. Reinsert drawer to continue cooking. Garnish with chopped fresh basil before serving.

Starters & Sides

Potato Gratin

Serves : 4 **Prep Time : 10 Mins** **Cook Time : 35 Mins**

Ingredients

- 1 kg Maris Piper potatoes, peeled and thinly sliced
- 1 tsp garlic powder
- 250ml double cream
- 150ml milk
- 250g grated cheddar cheese
- 2 tbsp butter
- Salt and pepper to taste

Recipe tip:

- It's important to slice the potatoes in the same thickness so that they cook at the same time.
- For extra texture, consider adding a crunchy topping before cooking. Mix some breadcrumbs with grated Parmesan and a sprinkle of your favourite herbs. Sprinkle over the potatoes, It'll add a delightful bit of crunch.

Preparation

1. Grease the Zone 1 and 2 drawers, and layer potatoes in the drawers (ends should overlapping slightly). Season each layer with salt, garlic powder and pepper, then spread 4 tbsp of cream and 2 tbsp milk on top and finally add a thin layer of grated Cheddar on top. Repeat layering in two drawers. Brush the final layer with melted butter.

2. In a bowl, add remaining cream and milk, mix and pour over the potatoes in both drawers.

3. Insert drawers in the unit. Select Zone 1, select AIR FRY, set temperature to 160°C and set time to 35 minutes. Select MATCH. Press START/STOP to begin.

4. When the cooking is complete, allow to set for 5 minutes before serving.

28

Starters & Sides

Broccoli and Cauliflower Cheese

Serves : 4   Prep Time : 10 Mins   Cook Time : 32 Mins

Ingredients

- 500g broccoli florets
- 500g cauliflower florets
- 1 tbsp oil
- 70g butter
- 4 tbsp plain flour
- 1 tsp garlic powder
- 200ml double cream
- 260ml milk
- 220g grated Cheddar
- Pinch of nutmeg
- Salt and pepper to taste

Recipe Variation:

Not a fan of broccoli in your cauliflower cheese? No worries! Simply follow the same recipe, but ditch the broccoli and double up on the cauliflower florets (instead of using just 500g cauliflower florets, add in a whole kilo!).

Preparation

1. In a bowl, add cauliflower, broccoli, oil, salt and pepper. Mix.

2. Insert the crisper plates in zone 1 and 2 drawers. Arrange the cauliflower and broccoli florets on the plates. Insert drawers in the unit.

3. Select Zone 1, select Roast, set temperature to 200°C and set time to 12 minutes. Select MATCH. Press START/STOP to begin.

4. In a saucepan, melt the butter over medium heat. Once melted, whisk in the flour. Cook for 1-2 minutes, stirring constantly, until golden brown. Gradually whisk in milk and cream, stirring constantly. Cook until the sauce thickens.

5. Remove the saucepan from the heat and stir in Cheddar , garlic powder, and nutmeg until melted and smooth. Season with and pepper.

6. Divide the cauliflower and broccoli florets between two casserole dishes. Pour the cheese sauce evenly over the broccoli and cauliflower, ensuring that all the florets are coated.

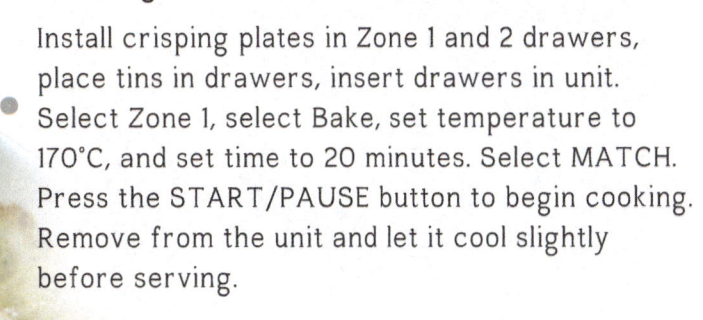

7. Install crisping plates in Zone 1 and 2 drawers, place tins in drawers, insert drawers in unit. Select Zone 1, select Bake, set temperature to 170°C, and set time to 20 minutes. Select MATCH. Press the START/PAUSE button to begin cooking. Remove from the unit and let it cool slightly before serving.

Starters & Sides

Courgette Pizza

Serves : 4   Prep Time : 10 Mins   Cook Time : 8 Mins

Ingredients

- 1 medium courgette, cut into 1/2-cm slices
- 110g pizza sauce/pizza topper
- 100g grated mozzarella cheese
- Pepperoni slices
- Salt and pepper to taste

Courgette Pizza Variation:

These courgette pizza bites are customisable and can be topped with your favourite pizza toppings. Add on some sliced cherry tomatoes, a few olives, some chopped peppers (any colour you like!), mushrooms, or even some leftover, chopped chicken.

Preparation

1. Sprinkle the courgette slices with salt and pepper.

2. Insert the crisper plates in zone 1 and 2 drawers. Brush plates with oil. Arrange the courgette slices on the plates.

3. Select Zone 1, select AIR FRY, set temperature to 180°C and set time to 6 minutes. Select MATCH. Press START/STOP to begin.

4. When the cooking is complete, top each slice with pizza topper, cheese, and pepperoni.

5. Reinsert drawers. Select Zone 1, select AIR FRY, set temperature to 180°C and set time to 7 minutes. Select MATCH. Press START/STOP to begin.
When cooking is complete, allow the courgette bites to cool slightly before serving.

Starters & Sides

Yorkshire Pudding

Serves : 12 yorkies **Prep Time : 35 Mins** **Cook Time : 12 Mins**

Ingredients

- 120g plain flour
- ¼ tsp salt
- 2 eggs
- 120ml milk
- 6 tsp sunflower oil

Recipe tip:

- Make sure all your ingredients (flour, eggs, and milk) are at room temperature. This helps ensure a lovely smooth batter and better rise.
- Use muffin tins with deep wells for best results. Shallow tins won't allow the puds to rise as high.
- Mix the batter until just combined. If you mix it too much, you'll be working the gluten in the flour, and that leads to tough puds instead of light and fluffy ones.

Preparation

1. In a large bowl, add flour, salt and mix. Add eggs, milk. Whisk until combined and smooth. Allow to rest for 30 minutes.

2. Add 1/2 tsp of oil into 12 individual muffin tins. Insert the crisper plates in zone 1 and 2 drawers. Place 6 tins on each crisper plate.

3. Select Zone 1, select ROAST, set temperature to 200°C and set time to 5 minutes. Select MATCH. Press START/STOP to begin.

4. When cooking is complete, remove drawers from unit and carefully fill each tin with batter ⅓ way full. Reinsert drawers to unit.

5. Select Zone 1, select BAKE, set temperature to 190°C and set time to 12 minutes. Select MATCH. Press START/STOP to begin.
When the cooking is complete, use silicone coated tongs to remove the yorkies to a serving dish and serve.

Starters & Sides

Cotswold Dumplings

Serves : 4   Prep Time : 35 Mins   Cook Time : 13 Mins

Ingredients

- 50g butter, softened
- 110g grated cheddar cheese
- 2 medium eggs, beaten
- 4 tsp milk
- 150g fresh (soft) breadcrumbs
- 3 tbsp dried breadcrumbs
- Salt and pepper to taste

Preparation

1. In a large bowl, add butter, cheese and whisk until combined. Add milk, eggs, salt, pepper and whisk. Add fresh breadcrumbs, mix. Shape mixture into 16 balls, then roll in the dried breadcrumbs. Cover and place in the fridge for 30 minutes.

2. Insert the crisper plates in zone 1 and 2 drawers. Place 8 balls on each crisper plate. Sprinkle/spray the balls with oil.

3. Select Zone 1, select AIR FRY, set temperature to 180°C and set time to 13 minutes. Select MATCH. Press START/STOP to begin.

4. When time reaches 7 minutes, remove drawers from unit and shake drawers. Reinsert drawers to continue cooking.

5. When the cooking is complete, use silicone coated tongs to remove the dumplings to a serving dish and serve.

Salami and Cheese Loaded Chips

Serves : 4   Prep Time : 10 Mins   Cook Time : 25 Mins

Ingredients

- 1 kg King Edward or Maris Piper potatoes, peeled and cut into 1-cm thin chips
- 1 tsp dried rosemary
- 2 tbsp oil
- 150g grated Cheddar
- 100g grated Mozzarella
- 150g salami slices
- 3 tbsp dried breadcrumbs
- Salt and pepper to taste

Loaded Chips Variation:

- Feel free to customise the toppings based on your preferences. Add diced bell peppers, caramelised onions, cooked sausage bits, or even pickled jalapeños.
- **Loaded Breakfast chips:** Serve loaded chips for breakfast by topping them with scrambled eggs, sausage pieces, cheddar cheese, diced tomatoes, and a sprinkle of chopped chives.

Preparation

1. Soak in the potatoes cold water for 30 minutes.

2. Drain the potatoes. Add oil, rosemary to the potatoes and mix until potatoes coated with oil.

3. Insert the crisper plates in both drawers. Place potatoes in Zone 1 and 2 drawers.

4. Select Zone 1, select AIR FRY, set temperature to 200°C and set time to 20 minutes. Select MATCH. Press START/STOP to begin. Shaking the drawers every 5 mins.

5. When the cooking is complete, open drawers, and top the potatoes with cheese and salami slices. Reinsert drawers.

6. Select Zone 1, select MAX CRISP and set time to 5 minutes. Select MATCH. Press START/STOP to begin. serve the chips with a side of sour cream for dipping.

Starters & Sides

Sausage Rolls

Serves : 4   Prep Time : 15 Mins   Cook Time : 15 Mins

Ingredients

- 6 sausages, casing removed
- 1 tsp English mustard
- 1 garlic clove, minced
- 4 tbsp breadcrumbs
- 1 tsp dried thyme
- 320g ready rolled puff pastry
- 1 egg mixed with 4 tbsp milk
- Sesame seeds
- Salt and pepper to taste

Preparation

1. In a bowl, add sausage-meat, thyme, mustard, garlic, breadcrumbs, salt, and pepper, then mix with hands until combined.

2. On a floured surface, lay pastry and cut it lengthways to 2 long rectangles. Roll the meat into sausage shapes and lay it in the center of each rectangle.

3. Brush pastry edge with egg/water mixture, then fold one side of pastry over, wrapping the filling inside. Press down with edge of a spoon to seal. Cut into pieces and brush the top with egg wash. Sprinkle with sesame seeds.

4. Insert the crisper plates in zone 1 and 2 drawers. Brush plates with oil. Place sausage rolls on crisper plates. Select Zone 1, select AIR FRY, set temperature to 180°C and set time to 15 minutes. Select MATCH. Press START/STOP to begin. Flipping after 12 minutes of cooking time.

5. When the cooking is complete, use silicone coated tongs to remove the sausage rolls to a serving dish. Serve immediately.

Recipe tip:

- Ensure your pastry dough remains cold throughout the process. That's what gives you lovely flaky layers when it bakes.
- Love a bit of extra cheese? Add a good handful of grated cheddar, Gouda, or Parmesan into your sausage meat for an oozy filling.

Dinners & Suppers

Featuring some of UK's most popular dinner and supper recipes

Sausage and Courgette Pasta Bake

Serves : 4 **Prep Time : 5 Mins** **Cook Time : 38 Mins**

Ingredients

- 4 Sausages, chopped
- 1 tbsp oil
- 1 medium onion, finely chopped
- 2 garlic cloves, minced
- 220g penne pasta
- 1 (400g) tin chopped tomatoes
- 1 medium courgette, grated
- 1 tsp dried oregano
- 500ml chicken stock
- Salt and pepper to taste

Preparation

1. With no crisping plate installed, add all ingredients to Zone 1 drawer. Stir to combine. Insert drawer into the unit.

2. Select zone 1, select BAKE, set temperature to 170°C, and set time to 38 minutes. Press the START/STOP button to begin cooking. Stir the pasta every 10 minutes.

3. When cooking is complete, stir then serve.

Recipe tip:

For cheesy, crunchy topping: Scatter some grated cheddar and handful of breadcrumbs over the top of the pasta bake and BAKE at 180°C for 5 minutes, until the cheese is golden brown and bubbly.

Beef Mains

Meatballs with Tomato Sauce

Serves : 4 Prep Time : 10 Mins Cook Time : 25 Mins

Ingredients

- 500g beef mince
- 75g breadcrumbs
- 2 tbsp grated Parmesan
- 1 large egg
- 4 garlic cloves, minced (divided)
- 1 tsp dried thyme
- Salt and pepper to taste
- 400g tin chopped tomato or Passata
- 1 tbsp Worcestershire sauce
- ¼ tsp dried oregano
- 1 small onion, finely chopped
- 50ml water

Preparation

1. In a bowl, add mince, breadcrumbs, Parmesan, egg, 2 garlic cloves, thyme, salt and pepper. Mix until combined.

2. Form the meatballs with two tablespoons of the beef mixture for each ball.

3. Install a crisping plate in the Zone 1 drawer, then place meatballs in the drawer and insert drawer in unit.

4. With no crisping plate installed, place the chopped tomato, 2 garlic cloves, Worcestershire sauce, onion, oregano, salt and pepper in the Zone 2 drawer and stir.

5. Select Zone 1, select AIR FRY, set temperature to 200°C, and set time to 10 minutes. Select Zone 2, select BAKE, set temperature to 180°C and set time for 25 minutes. Press the START/PAUSE button to begin cooking.

6. When cooking time in Zone 1 time complete, remove drawer from unit and transfer the meatballs into zone 2 drawer with the tomato mixture and stir gently. Reinsert drawer to continue cooking. When the cooking is complete, serve meatballs with rice.

Beef Mains

Rosemary Garlic Lamb Chops

Serves : 4   Prep Time : 15 Mins   Cook Time : 15 Mins

Ingredients

- 600g lamb chops
- 2 tbsp oil
- 3 rosemary sprigs
- 2 thyme sprigs
- 3 garlic cloves, minced
- Salt and pepper to taste

Recipe tip:

Serve the lamb chops with side dishes such as roasted vegetables, potato mash, or a fresh salad.

Lamb Chops Variation:

Want to add a bit of freshness?
Swap out the rosemary and thyme for fresh mint. The lamb and mint combo is a classic for a reason!

Preparation

1. In a bowl, add oil, rosemary, thyme, garlic, salt, and pepper. Mix until all lamb chops coated with seasoning. Set aside for 15 minutes.

2. Insert crisper plates in zone 1 and 2 drawers. Brush with oil. Place the lamb chops in an even layer into each drawer. Insert drawers in unit. Select zone 1, select AIR FRY, set temperature to 180°C and set time to 15 minutes. Select MATCH. Press START/STOP to begin. (When time reaches 8 minutes, remove drawers from unit and flip the chops. Reinsert drawers to continue cooking).

3. When cooking is complete, remove both drawers from the unit and remove the lamb chops from and allow to rest for 5 minutes before serving.

Sausage and Peppers

Serves : 6   Prep Time : 5 Mins   Cook Time : 17 Mins

Ingredients

- 3 bell peppers , sliced
- 1 large onion, sliced
- 1 tbsp oil
- 6 sausages
- Salt and pepper to taste
- 6 of your favourite buns

Recipe tip:

These sausage and peppers aren't just for sandwiches! Serve over some cooked pasta, fluffy rice, or a creamy potato mash.

Preparation

1. In a bowl, add all ingredients (except buns) and mix.

2. Insert crisper plates in zone 1 and 2 drawers. Divide the sausage mixture into drawers. Insert drawers in unit. Select zone 1, select AIR FRY, set temperature to 200°C and set time to 17 minutes. Select MATCH. Press START/STOP to begin. (When time reaches 10 minutes, remove drawers from unit and shake drawers. Reinsert drawers to continue cooking).

3. When cooking is complete, remove drawers from unit. Divide the onion and peppers between the buns, then place one sausages in each bun and serve

Beef Mains

Haggis Burger

Serves : 6   **Prep Time : 5 Mins**   **Cook Time : 8 mins**

Ingredients

- 300g haggis
- 300g beef mince
- 120g grated Cheddar
- Salt and pepper to taste

Recipe tip:

Lightly toast the burger buns to add a nice crunch and prevent them from becoming soggy from the juicy haggis patty and toppings.

Preparation

1. In a bowl add all ingredients and mix with hand until combined. Divide mixture into 6 portions. Roll and press together, then flatten slightly.

2. Insert a crisper plates in both drawers. Place burgers in Zone 1 and Zone 2 drawers, then insert drawers in unit.

3. Select zone 1, select AIR FRY, set temperature to 190°C and set time to 8 minute. Select MATCH. Select START/STOP to begin.

4. When Zone 1 time reaches 4 minutes, remove drawers from unit and flip burgers. Reinsert drawers to continue cooking.

5. When cooking is complete, remove from unit. Serve with with your favourite toppings (lettuce, tomato, and sauces you like).

Beef Mains

Lamb Burgers

Serves : 4   Prep Time : 5 Mins   Cook Time : 12 Mins

Ingredients

- 500g lamb mince
- 2 garlic cloves, minced
- 1 medium onion, grated
- 2 tbsp chopped mint leaves
- Salt and pepper to taste
- Burger buns
- Lettuce, tomato slices, red onion slices (for serving)

Recipe tip:

- When mixing the ingredients, avoid overmixing the lamb mixture. Use your hands to gently combine the ingredients until just mixed. Overmixing makes dense burgers.
- Use your thumb to make a gentle dip in the centre of each patty. It stops the burgers from puffing up in the middle while they cook.

Preparation

1. In a bowl, add all ingredients and mix.

2. Divide mixture into 4 equal portions. Roll each portion into a ball and then flatten it.

3. Add the burgers in a single layer in zone 1 & 2 drawers (with crisper plate inserted), then insert drawers in unit. Select zone 1, select AIR FRY, set temperature to 180°C and set time to 12 minutes. Select MATCH. Press START/STOP to begin.

4. When time reaches 7 minutes, remove drawers from unit and flip the burgers. Reinsert drawers to continue cooking.

5. When cooking is complete, assemble the burgers by placing a lamb patty on the bottom half of each bun. Top with lettuce, tomato slices, red onion slices, and any other desired toppings such as sliced cheese, or pickles.

Beef Mains

Popeseye Steak with Garlic Dill Butter

Serves : 4   Prep Time : 10 Mins   Cook Time : 15 Mins

Ingredients

For the dill butter
- 120g butter, softened
- 2 tbsp dill, finely chopped
- 2 garlic cloves, minced

For the Popeseye steak
- 4 (150g each) Rump/popeseye Steaks, room temperature
- 2 tbsp butter, softened
- Salt and pepper to taste

Recipe tip:
- If the rump steaks have a thick layer of fat along the edge, score it with a sharp knife. This helps the fat render out nicely as the steak cooks.
- Feel free to customise the garlic dill butter to your taste. Add additional herbs like parsley or chives, or other flavours like lemon zest, red pepper flakes, or Worcestershire sauce.

Preparation

1. In a bowl, add butter and mash with a fork. Add the minced garlic, dill and mix.

2. Transfer the garlic dill butter on a piece of clingfilm. Form it into a sausage shape and twist the ends to seal. Place in the fridge.

3. Pat dry the steaks with kitchen paper. Rub steaks with 2 tbsp softened butter and season both sides with salt and pepper.

4. Place the steaks in Zone 1 and 2 drawers (with crisper plate inserted), then insert drawers in unit. Select zone 1, Select AIR FRY, set temperature to 200°C and set time to 13 minutes. Select MATCH. Press START/STOP to begin.

5. When time reaches 7 minutes, remove drawers from unit and flip the steaks. Reinsert drawers to continue cooking.
When cooking is complete, transfer the steak to a plate, top with garlic dill butter, cover with foil and rest for 5 mins. Serve.

Beef Mains

Barnsley Chops with Mint Sauce

Serves : 2   Prep Time : 40 Mins   Cook Time : 13 Mins

Ingredients

- 2 (350g each) Barnsley/saddle chops
- 2 tbsp oil
- Salt and pepper to taste
- 2 tsp chopped rosemary
- 2 tbsp butter

For the mint sauce:

- Handful fresh mint leaves, finely chopped
- 2 tbsp white vinegar
- 1 tbsp caster sugar
- 2 tbsp boiling water

Recipe tip:

- You can prepare the mint sauce in advance and store it in the fridge until ready to serve.

Preparation

1. In a shallow dish rub chops with oil and then sprinkle with the chopped rosemary. Cover and refrigerate for 30 mins.

2. Remove the chops out of the fridge and set aside until reaches room temperature. Sprinkle the chops with salt and pepper.

3. Place the chops in Zone 1 and 2 drawers (with crisper plate inserted), then insert drawers in unit. Select Zone, Select AIR FRY, set temperature to 200°C and set time to 13 minutes. Select MATCH. Press START/STOP to begin. Flipping after 7 minutes.

4. In a small bowl, combine the chopped mint leaves, vinegar, sugar, and boiling water. Stir until the sugar is dissolved. Set aside.

5. When cooking is complete, transfer chops to a plate and top with butter and loosely cover with tin foil for 5 minutes before serving. Serve the Barnsley chops, with the mint sauce.

Beef Mains

Mustard Glazed Tomahawk Steak with Garlic and Parsley Sauce

Serves : 4   Prep Time : 10 Mins   Cook Time : 25 Mins

Ingredients

- 1 kg Tomahawk steak, room temperature
- 2 tbsp butter
- Salt and pepper to taste
- 1 tbsp wholegrain mustard

For the Garlic Parsley Sauce:

- 1 tbsp Balsamic Vinegar
- 3 garlic cloves, minced
- 1 Punch fresh flat leaf parsley, finely chopped
- 120ml olive oil
- Salt and pepper to taste

Preparation

1. Season steak on both sides with salt and pepper.

2. Place the steak in zone 1 drawer (with crisper plate inserted), then insert drawer in unit. Select zone 1, select ROAST, set temperature to 190°C and set time to 15 minutes. (For medium rare: cook for 15 mins . For rare: cook for 12 mins).

3. When time reaches 7 minutes, remove drawer from unit and flip the steak. Reinsert drawer to continue cooking.

4. When cooking is complete, remove drawer and brush steak with mustard. Reinsert drawers. Select ROAST, set temp to 190°C and set time to 10 min. Press START/ STOP button to begin cooking. Flipping after 5 minutes.

5. When cooking is complete, remove steak, transfer to a plate and top with butter. Loosely cover the steak with foil in a warm place, for 5 minutes.

6. In a bowl, add all sauce ingredients and mix until combined. Slice steak and serve with sauce.

Recipe tip:

Use a thermometer to check the internal temperature of the steak for perfect doneness. For medium-rare (54-57 °C). For medium (57-63 °C). For medium-well (63-68 °C). For well-done, (68-74 °C).

Beef Mains

Cheesesteak Sub Rolls

Serves : 4 **Prep Time : 10 Mins** **Cook Time : 13 Mins**

Ingredients

- 500g sirloin steak, thinly sliced
- 2 tbsp Worcestershire sauce
- 2 tbsp oil
- 1 garlic clove, minced
- 1 large onion, thinly sliced
- 2 green bell pepper, sliced
- 4 Red Leicester slices
- Salt and pepper to taste

Recipe Variation:

- Spread a generous amount of horseradish cream sauce on the inside of the sub roll before adding the beef and cheese.
- **Stilton and Mushroom Cheesesteak Sub Roll:** Add sautéed mushrooms and crumbled Stilton cheese to the sandwich for a gourmet twist.

Preparation

1. In a bowl, add the onions, peppers and 1 tbsp oil and mix. In another bowl, add beef slices, 1 tbsp oil, garlic powder, Worcestershire sauce and mix.

2. Place the beef slices in zone 1 drawer (with crisper plate inserted). Place the onion mixture in zone 2 drawer (with no crisper plate inserted), then insert drawers in unit.

3. Select zone 1, select AIR FRY, set temperature to 190°C and set time to 12 minutes. Select Zone 2, select ROAST, set temperature to 160°C and set time for 13 minutes. Select SYNC. Press the START/PAUSE button to begin cooking.

4. When cooking time reaches 6 minutes, remove drawers, stir the onion mixture and flip the beef slices. Reinsert drawer to continue cooking.

5. When cooking is complete, divide the cooked steak evenly among the rolls, then top with the **onions and peppers** mixture. Place a slice of **cheese on top of** each sandwich.

6. Return the sandwiches to the drawers and AIR FRY at 200°C for an additional 2-3 minutes until the cheese is melted.

Beef Mains

Stuffed Saddle of Lamb

Serves : 4   Prep Time : 15 Mins   Cook Time : 50 mins

Ingredients

- 1 kg boneless saddle or leg of lamb (butterflied), room temperature
- 2 onions, cut into thick slices
- 1 tsp Wholegrain Mustard
- Salt and pepper to taste
- 2 tbsp oil

For the stuffing:

- 1 tbsp thyme, finely chopped
- 2 garlic cloves, minced
- 1 tbsp parsley, finely chopped
- 1 tbsp rosemary, finely chopped
- zest and juice of 1 lemon
- 100g breadcrumbs
- 1 handful pine nuts
- Salt and pepper to taste

Recipe tip:

Use a thermometer to check the internal temperature of the lamb for perfect doneness. Medium-rare (60-65°C), Medium (65–70°C) and Medium well done (70°C)

Preparation

1. In a large bowl, add all the stuffing ingredients and mix until combined.

2. Place the saddle of lamb skin side down on a cutting board. Scoop the stuffing into the middle of the saddle.

3. Cut 4 pieces of string about 15-cm longer than the saddle of lamb. Roll up the lamb and tie with the strings.

4. Insert the crisper plate in Zone 1 drawer. Place onion on crisper plate. Then Put lamb on top of onions and rub with oil and . Season with salt and pepper.

5. Select Zone 1, select ROAST, set temperature to 190°C and set time to 20 minutes. Press START/STOP to begin.

6. When cooking time is complete in Zone 1 drawer, flip the lamb, turn the heat down to 170°C and Continue to ROAST for 30 minutes.

7. When cooking is complete, remove the lamb from the unit. Loosely cover with foil in a warm place, for 20 minutes. Slice and serve.

Beef Mains

Beef Bites and Gravy

Serves : 4-6   Prep Time : 5 Mins   Cook Time : 35 mins

Ingredients

- 500g diced beef, cut into small cubes
- 2 tbsp oil
- 1 onion, finely chopped
- 2 garlic cloves, minced
- 225g mushroom, sliced
- 500ml hot beef stock
- 2 tbsp Worcestershire sauce
- 1 bay leaf
- 1 tbsp tomato paste
- Salt and pepper to taste

To Thicken Gravy:

- 1 tbsp cornflour mixed with 1 tbsp water

Preparation

1. With no crisping plate installed, place all ingredients (except cornflour/water mixture) in the Zone 1 drawer. Stir to combine.

2. Select Zone 1, select AIR FRY, set temperature to 200°C, and set time to 35 minutes. Press the START/PAUSE button to begin cooking. Stirring every 10 minutes.

3. When the cooking is complete, remove drawer and stir, add the cornflour/water mixture and stir until thickened .
Serve with pasta, rice or potato mash.

Beef Mains

Scotch Eggs

Serves : 6   Prep Time : 15 Mins   Cook Time : 15 mins

Ingredients

- 6 eggs, boiled and peeled
- 400g sausage, casing removed
- 4 tbsp plain flour
- 1/2 tsp garlic powder
- 1 large egg
- 120 g breadcrumbs
- 1/2 tsp smoked paprika
- Salt and pepper to taste

Recipe tip:

Add flavuor to the sausage meat by adding fresh herbs, or spices like grated cheese, Worcestershire sauce, dried thyme or chopped fresh sage

Preparation

1. In a bowl, add the flour and season with salt, pepper and garlic powder. In another bowl, add the egg and whisk. In a third bowl, add breadcrumbs, smoked paprika and mix.

2. Divide the sausage meat into 6 equal balls. On a working surface lined with baking paper, flatten each ball into a thin round patty enough to wrap an egg.

3. Place one egg in the centre of each sausage meat and wrap it around the egg. Roll each covered egg in flour then in the egg and then roll in breadcrumbs.

4. Insert the crisper plates in zone 1 and 2 drawers. Place Scotch eggs on crisper plate and spray with oil. Select AIR FRY, set temperature to 190°C and set time to 15 minutes. Select MATCH. Press START/STOP to begin. Flipping every 5 minutes.

5. When the cooking is complete, use silicone coated tongs to remove the scotch eggs to a serving dish. Serve with a salad, and chips.

Beef Mains

Shepherd's Pie

Serves : 4 **Prep Time : 10 Mins** **Cook Time : 30 mins**

Ingredients

Topping:
- 400g mashed potatoes
- 60ml milk
- 3 tbsp melted butter
- 100g grated cheddar cheese

Filling:
- 1 onion, finely chopped
- 2 garlic cloves, minced
- 500g lamb mince
- 150g frozen peas and carrots
- 1 tbsp tomato puree
- 100ml hot beef stock
- 2 tsp Worcestershire sauce
- ½ tsp dried thyme
- Salt and pepper to taste

Preparation

1. In a bowl, add all topping ingredients, season with salt, pepper. Mix until combined, set aside.

2. With no crisping plate installed, place all filling ingredients in the Zone 1 drawer, season with salt and pepper. Stir to combine.

3. Select Zone 1, select AIR FRY, set temperature to 200°C, and set time to 16 minutes. Press the START/PAUSE button to begin cooking.

4. When time reaches 10 minutes, remove drawer from unit and stir. Reinsert drawer to continue cooking.

5. When cooking is complete, remove drawer from unit. Top the mince with the potato mash mixture. Insert both drawers into unit.

6. Select Zone 1, select BAKE, set temperature to 190°C and set time to 14 minutes. Press START/STOP to begin.
Let the shepherd's pie rest for 10 minutes before serving.

Recipe tip:

For a proper golden brown, crispy topping: Spread the mashed potatoes evenly over the meat filling. Using a fork, create ridges on the surface of the potatoes, which will become golden and crispy.
Or sprinkle some grated Cheddar on top of the mash before baking.

Beef Mains

Mini Beef Wellingtons

Serves : 4   **Prep Time : 13 Mins**   **Cook Time : 16 mins**

Ingredients

- 200g mushrooms, finely chopped
- 2 garlic cloves, minced
- 2 tbsp butter
- 450g rump steaks, cut into 5-cm cubes
- 1 tbsp oil
- 320g Ready rolled puff pastry
- 3 tbsp English mustard
- 1 egg, lightly beaten
- Salt and pepper to taste

Recipe tip:

Seal the edges of the puff pastry tightly around the beef to prevent the filling from leaking out during baking.

Preparation

1. In a pan over medium-high heat, sauté the mushrooms and garlic in butter until the liquid has evaporated. Season with salt and pepper. Season the steak cubes with salt and pepper and brush with oil.

2. Place the steak cubes in zone 1 and 2 drawers (with crisper plate inserted), then insert drawers in unit. Select ROAST, set temperature to 190°C and set time to 6 minutes. Select MATCH. Press START/STOP to begin. Flipping after 3 minutes.

3. When the cooking is complete, transfer the steak cubes to a plate. Set aside.

4. On a lightly floured surface, lay the pastry sheet and cut vertically into three equal strips. Cut each strip into 5 squares. Brush with mustard.

5. Spread some of the mushroom on each pastry square, then place a steak cube on top of each mushroom-covered squares.

6. Wrap the pastry around each steak cube, sealing the edges and brush all over with the beaten egg.

7. Place the beef wellingtons in zone 1 and 2 drawers (with crisper plate inserted), insert drawers in unit. Select AIR FRY, set temperature to 190°C and set time to 10 minutes. Select MATCH. Press START/STOP to begin cooking. Flipping after 8 minutes.

8. When the cooking is complete, transfer into a plate and allow to rest for a few minutes before serving.

Beef Mains

Toad In The Hole

Serves : 4 Prep Time : 10 Mins Cook Time : 27 mins

Ingredients

- 250g plain flour
- 2 large eggs
- 250g whole milk
- 1 tbsp English mustard
- 2 tbsp oil or melted butter
- 8 small English sausages
- Salt and pepper to taste

Recipe tip:

- Mix the batter until just combined. If you mix it too much, you'll be activating the gluten in the flour, and that leads to tough toads in the hole instead of light and fluffy one.
- Cook the toad in the hole directly in the drawer without using silicone liners. This ensures even cooking and a crispy crust.

Preparation

1. In a bowl, add flour, salt and pepper. Add the eggs and milk and mix until combined and smooth. (If it's too thick, add more milk). Cover and set aside.

2. With no crisping plate installed, place the sausages in zone 1 and 2 drawers, add 1 tbsp butter or oil in each drawer, then insert drawers in unit. Select AIR FRY, set temperature to 200°C and set time to 10 minutes. Select MATCH. Press START/STOP to begin cooking.

4. When cooking is complete, remove drawers from unit and carefully pour in the batter on top of the oil and sausages. Insert drawers into unit.

5. Select Zone 1, select BAKE, set temperature to 180°C and set time to 17 minutes. Select MATCH. Press START/STOP to begin cooking. When Zone 1 time reaches 13 minutes, remove drawers from unit and flip the toad in the hole using a spatula. Reinsert drawers to continue cooking.
When cooking is complete, transfer into plates and serve.

Beef Mains

Forfar Bridie

Serves : 6 **Prep Time : 40 Mins** **Cook Time : 40 mins**

Ingredients

For the shortcrust pastry:
- 450g plain flour
- 225g cold butter, cut into small cubes
- Pinch of salt
- Cold water, as needed

For the filling:
- 450g beef skirt steak, cut into 1-cm cubes
- 1 onion, finely chopped
- 1/2 tsp mustard powder
- 1 tbsp plain flour
- Salt and pepper to taste
- 1 egg, whisked (for brushing)

Recipe Variation:
To turn these Forfar Bridies into Cornish Pasties, simply add finely diced potatoes and swede to the meat filling before assembling the pastries.

Preparation

1. In a bowl, add filling ingredients, mix and set aside.

2. In a bowl, add flour, salt. Mix. Add the butter, and rub with hands into the flour until mixture resembles breadcrumbs. Add water gradually while mixing until a dough comes together (Do Not overmix). Shape into a ball, cover with clingfilm and refrigerate for 30 Minutes.

3. Divide pastry into 6 balls. Transfer into a floured surface, then roll out each ball into 15-cm circle.

4. Fill each pastry circle with filling mixture on one side of each circle and brush edges with beaten egg. Fold top half of the pasty over the filling and seal around the edges. Brush tops with egg.

5. Insert crisper plates in both drawers. Place 3 Bridies in each drawer, then insert drawers in unit.

6. Select Zone 1, select AIR FRY, set temperature to 160°C, and set time to 40 minutes. Select MATCH. Press the START/PAUSE button to begin cooking. (flipping after 20 minutes. If they start to get too brown, cover with foil).

7. When cooking is complete, transfer to a plate. let cool for 10 minutes before serving.

Roasted Leg of Lamb and Potatoes

Serves : 4   Prep Time : 10 Mins   Cook Time : 50 mins

Ingredients

- Half lamb leg
- 4 tbs oil
- 600g Maris Piper or King Edwards potatoes, peeled and cut into cubes or quarters
- 1 tbsp garlic powder
- 1 tbsp smoked paprika
- 1 tbsp dried thyme
- 1 tbsp dried rosemary
- Salt and pepper to taste

Recipe tip:

- Before roasting, bring the lamb leg to room temperature.
- Cut your potatoes into similar-sized pieces to ensure even cooking
- For extra crispy roast potatoes, parboil them before tossing them in oil and roasting.

Preparation

1. Soak potatoes in cold water for 30 minutes. Drain, then pat with a paper towel until very dry.

2. Season the potatoes with smoked paprika, 2 tbsp oil, salt and pepper. Mix until potatoes coated with seasoning.

3. Rub the lamb leg with 2 tbsp oil, garlic powder, thyme, rosemary, season with salt and pepper.

4. Insert a crisper plates in both drawers. Place lamb leg in zone 1 drawer. Place potatoes in zone 2 drawer, then insert drawers in unit.

5. Select zone 1, select ROAST, set temperature to 170°C and set time to 50 minute. Select zone 2, select AIR FRY, set temperature to 200°C, and set time to 25 minutes. Select START/STOP to begin.

6. When Zone 2 time reaches 10 minutes, remove drawer from unit and shake drawer. When Zone 1 time reaches 25 minutes, remove drawer from unit and flip the lamb leg.

7. When cooking is complete, remove the lamb and let it rest before slicing. (The lamb is cooked when its internal temperature reaches 63°C). Serve lamb with potato.

Minced Beef and Cheddar Bake

Serves : 4 **Prep Time : 5 Mins** **Cook Time : 30 mins**

Ingredients

- 450g beef mince
- 1 large onion, chopped
- 3 garlic cloves, minced
- 350g tomato pasta sauce
- 1 small carrot, peeled and finely chopped
- 300g cooked rice
- 1 celery stalk, thinly sliced
- 60g grated cheddar cheese
- 60g grated mozzarella
- Salt and pepper to taste

Recipe Variation:

Fancy a bit of pasta instead of rice ? Simply stir in cooked pasta with that lovely minced beef and tomato mixture. Chuck on a good layer of cheddar and mozzarella, bake as per the recipe

Preparation

1. With no crisping plate installed, place mince, onion, garlic, carrot, celery in the Zone 1 drawer, season with salt and peeper. Stir to combine.

2. Select Zone 1, select AIR FRY, set temperature to 180°C, and set time to 15 minutes. Press the START/PAUSE button to begin cooking

3. When time reaches 8 minutes, remove drawer from unit and stir. Reinsert drawer to continue cooking.

4. When cooking is complete, remove drawer from unit and drain any fat. Top the mince with the rice, tomato sauce, salt and pepper, stir gently. Sprinkle with cheddar and mozzarella. Insert drawer into unit.

5. Select zone 1, select BAKE, set temperature to 200°C and set time to 15 minutes. Press START/STOP to begin. When cooking is complete, serve.

Chicken Mains

Lemon Garlic Chicken and Orzo

Serves : 4 **Prep Time : 5 Mins** **Cook Time : 30 mins**

Ingredients

- 4 bone-in, skin-on chicken thighs
- 2 tbsp oil
- 1 tsp garlic powder
- 1 small onion, finely chopped
- 2 tbsp butter
- 250g dry orzo pasta
- 100g fresh spinach
- 2 garlic cloves, minced
- 600ml chicken stock
- Salt and pepper to taste

Recipe tip:

For a creamier texture, stir in a splash of double cream at the end of cooking. This adds richness and creaminess to the dish.

Preparation

1. Pat the chicken dry, season with salt and pepper and garlic powder.

2. Install a crisping plate in the Zone 1 drawer, then place chicken thighs in the drawer and insert drawer in unit.

3. With no crisping plate installed, place orzo, stock, spinach, garlic, butter and onions in the Zone 2 drawer and stir to combine.

4. Select Zone 1, select AIR FRY, set temperature to 200°C, and set time to 20 minutes. Select Zone 2, select BAKE, set temperature to 200°C and set time for 30 minutes. Select SYNC. Press the START/PAUSE button to begin cooking. Flip the chicken and stir the orzo halfway cooking time.

5. When cooking is complete, cover orzo with foil and leave to rest for 5 mins before serving. Serve chicken with orzo.

Lemon Thyme Roast Chicken

Serves : 4   Prep Time : 5 Mins   Cook Time : 1 Hour

Ingredients

- 1 whole chicken (about 1.6-2 kg)
- 3 tbsp soft butter
- 3 garlic cloves, minced
- Juice and zest of 1 large lemon
- 1 1/2 tsp dried thyme
- Salt and pepper to taste

Recipe tip:

- Make sure the butter mixture is evenly spread under the skin of the chicken.
- Feel free to add other herbs or spices to the butter mixture. Rosemary, or sage can be used in place of or in addition to thyme.
- For a Crispy skin MAX CRISP for 3 minutes.

Preparation

1. In a small bowl, mix together the butter, garlic, thyme, lemon zest, lemon juice, salt, and pepper.

2. Rub the butter all over the chicken, making sure to get it under the skin and into the cavity as well.

3. Install a crisping plate in the Zone 1 drawer, then place chicken in the drawer (breast side down) and insert drawer in unit.

4. Select Zone 1, select ROAST, set temperature to 180°C, and set time to 30 minutes. Press the START/PAUSE button to begin cooking.

5. When cooking is complete, flip the chicken and ROAST at 180°C for another 30 minutes. Once cooked, remove the chicken from the unit and let it rest for 10 minutes before slicing.

Chicken Pasties

🔔 Serves : 8   🥣 Prep Time : 20 Mins   📟 Cook Time : 35 mins

Ingredients

Pasties
- 500g plain flour
- 250g cold butter, cubed
- 1 egg, whisked (for brushing)
- Cold water, as needed

Filling
- 1 swede, finely chopped
- 1 onion, finely chopped
- 1 carrot, finely chopped
- 1 celery stalk, finely chopped
- 2 boneless and skinless chicken breasts, cut into 1-cm cubes
- 60g plain flour
- 120g grated cheddar
- 60ml melted butter
- Salt & pepper to taste
- 1 egg mixed with 1 tbsp water

Preparation

1. In a bowl, add filling ingredients, mix and set aside.

2. In a bowl, add flour, salt. Mix. Add butter, and rub with hands into flour until resembles breadcrumbs. Add water gradually while mixing until a dough comes together (Do Not over mix).

3. Divide dough into 8 balls. Transfer into a floured surface, then roll out each ball into 20-cm circle.

4. Fill each pastie with filling mixture on one side of each pastry circle and brush edges with beaten egg. Fold top half of the pasty down over the filling and seal around the edges. Brush tops with egg.

5. Insert crisper plates in both drawers. Place 4 chicken pasties in each drawer, then insert drawers in unit.

6. Select Zone 1, select BAKE, set temperature to 170°C, and set time to 30-35 minutes. Select MATCH. Press the START/PAUSE button to begin cooking

7. When time reaches 15 minutes, remove drawers from unit and flip the pasties. Reinsert drawers to continue cooking.
When cooking is complete, let cool for 5 minutes before serving.

Chicken Mains

Sweet & Sticky Chicken Kebabs

Serves : 4   Prep Time : 30 Mins   Cook Time : 15 Mins

Ingredients

- 500g boneless, skinless chicken thighs, cut into bite-sized pieces
- 3 tbsp soy sauce
- 2 tbsp runny honey
- 2 garlic cloves, minced
- 1 tsp grated ginger
- 1 tsp white vinegar
- 1 tsp onion powder
- 1 tsp smoked paprika
- Salt and pepper to taste
- Wooden skewers soaked in water

Recipe Variation:

You can use salmon instead of chicken, simply cut salmon fillet into chunks and marinate them. Thread the marinated salmon cubes onto skewers and and AIR FRY at 170°C for 11 minutes.

Preparation

1. In bowl, add all ingredients and mix until the chicken coated with spices. Cover with clingfilm and let marinade for at least 30 minutes in the fridge.

2. Thread the chicken thigh pieces onto the skewers, leaving a little space between each piece.

3. Insert the crisper plates in zone 1 and 2 drawers. Place the skewers on crisper plate and brush the with any remaining marinade. Select Zone 1, select AIR FRY, set temperature to 190°C and set time to 15 minutes. Select MATCH. Press START/STOP to begin. Flipping halfway cooking time.

4. When the cooking is complete, use silicone coated tongs to remove the skewers to a serving dish and let them rest for a few minutes before serving. Serve with rice, roasted vegetables, or a salad.

Chicken Mains

Stuffed Chicken Breast

Serves : 4   Prep Time : 10 Mins   Cook Time : 20 mins

Ingredients

- 4 medium, boneless and skinless chicken breasts
- 1 tbsp smoked paprika
- 1 tsp dried thyme
- 1 tbsp onion powder

For the filling:
- 60g pepperoni slices
- 150g mozzarella slices
- 100g grated cheddar
- Salt and pepper to taste

Recipe Variation:

Delicious filling variations you can try for stuffed chicken breast:
- Pesto sauce, sun-dried tomatoes, pine nuts and goat cheese.
- Sautéed mushrooms, spinach, garlic, and cream cheese. Season with salt, pepper, and a pinch of nutmeg.
- Sun-dried tomatoes, fresh basil leaves, and mozzarella cheese and a drizzle of balsamic vinegar.

Preparation

1. Make a slit in each chicken breast using a sharp knife. Season the chicken breasts with paprika, thyme, onion powder, salt and pepper.

2. Stuff each chicken breast with ¼ of the pepperoni slices, ¼ of the cheddar and 2 mozzarella slices (Use toothpicks to secure the stuffing).

3. Insert a crisper plate in both drawers. Place two chicken breasts in each drawer, sprinkle with oil, then insert drawers in unit.

4. Select Zone 1, select AIR FRY, set temperature to 200°C, and set time to 20 minutes. Select MATCH. Press the START/PAUSE button to begin cooking (The internal temperature of the chicken needs to reach 74°C to ensure that it's cooked).

5. When cooking is complete, let the chicken rest for 5 minutes before serving.

Chicken Mains

Glazed Chicken Thighs

Serves : 4   Prep Time : 1 Hour   Cook Time : 18-20 mins

Ingredients

- 4 bone-in, skin-on chicken thighs

For the glaze:
- ½ tsp chili powder
- 1 tsp mustard powder
- 1 garlic clove, minced
- 3 tbsp tomato sauce
- 1 tbsp grated fresh ginger
- 2 tsp Worcestershire sauce
- 1 tbsp oil
- Salt and pepper to taste

Preparation

1. In a large bowl, add all glaze ingredients and mix until combined. Place the chicken thighs into the bowl and cover with glaze.

2. Cover the bowl with clingfilm and refrigerate for an hour.

3. Add the chicken thighs in a single layer in Zone 1 and Zone 2 drawers (with crisper plate inserted). Brush the glaze evenly over the chicken thighs, covering them completely, then insert drawers in unit. Select zone 1, select ROAST, set temperature at 200°C for 18-20 mins (depending on the size of the thighs), Select MATCH. Press the START/PAUSE button to begin cooking.
Flipping after 10 minutes.
Serve with potato or salad.

Crispy Katsu Chicken

🔔 Serves : 4   🥣 Prep Time : 5 Mins   🍳 Cook Time : 13 mins

Ingredients

- 4 boneless, skinless, chicken breasts (160g each), flattened into 3-cm thick
- 40g plain flour
- 1/2 tsp garlic powder
- 150g Panko breadcrumbs
- 1 large egg
- Salt and pepper to taste

Katsu sauce:
- 1/2 tsp onion powder
- 1/4 tsp Curry Powder
- 1/4 tsp garlic powder
- 2 ½ tsp worcestershire sauce
- ½ tsp brown sugar
- 80ml ketchup
- 1 ½ tbsp Soy sauce

Preparation

1. Season the chicken breasts with salt, pepper and garlic powder.

2. In a bowl, beat the egg. In a second bowl, add the flour and season with salt and pepper. In a third bowl, add the breadcrumbs.
Dip each piece of chicken first in the flour, then in the egg, then finally the breadcrumbs.

3. Add the chicken in a single layer in Zone 1 and Zone 2 drawers (with crisper plate inserted). Drizzle or spray with oil, then insert drawers in unit. Select zone 1, select AIR FRY, set temperature at 200°C for 13 mins, Select MATCH. Press the START/PAUSE button to begin cooking. Flip the chicken and spray with oil halfway through cooking time.

4. In a small saucepan over low heat, combine the ketchup, Worcestershire sauce, soy sauce, sugar, onion powder, and garlic powder. Cook stirring occasionally, until the sauce is heated through and well combined. Remove from heat. Slice the chicken into strips or serve it whole, alongside the Katsu sauce.

Rosemary Chicken with Roasted Vegetables

Serves : 4 | **Prep Time : 5 Mins** | **Cook Time : 20-25 mins**

Ingredients

For the Chicken:
- 4 boneless chicken breasts
- 2 tbsp melted butter
- 1 tbsp chopped fresh rosemary
- 2 garlic cloves, minced
- Salt and pepper to taste

For the Roasted Vegetables:
- 400g mixed vegetables (such as bell peppers, courgettes, cherry tomatoes, and red onions), chopped into bite-sized pieces
- 1 tbsp balsamic vinegar
- 1 garlic clove, minced
- 1 tbsp oil
- Salt and pepper to taste

Preparation

1. In a bowl, add butter, rosemary, garlic, salt, pepper and mix until combined. Place the chicken breasts into the bowl and cover with spice mixture.

2. In a separate bowl, add the mixed vegetables, oil, garlic, balsamic vinegar salt, and pepper. Mix.

3. Add the chicken in a single layer in Zone 1 drawer (with crisper plate inserted). Add the mixed vegetables in Zone 2 drawer (with no crisper plate inserted), then insert drawers in unit. Select Zone 1, select ROAST, set temperature to 180°C, and set time to 20-25 minutes (depending on size). Select Zone 2, select ROAST, set temperature to 200°C and set time for 20 minutes. Select SYNC. Press the START/PAUSE button to begin cooking. Serve the rosemary chicken breasts with the roasted vegetables.

Recipe tip:
For extra flavour, marinate the chicken breasts in the rosemary mixture for at least 30 minutes before baking

Recipe Variation:
Herb and Mustard Crusted Chicken Breast: mix breadcrumbs, chopped fresh herbs like parsley and thyme, a tsp of English mustard, and a drizzle of oil. Spread this mixture over the chicken breasts, press and bake .

Chicken Mains

Crispy Chicken Breast Chunks

Serves : 4 | **Prep Time : 5 Mins** | **Cook Time : 11 mins**

Ingredients

- 4 boneless chicken breasts, cut into bite-sized pieces
- 1 tsp garlic powder
- 1 tsp onion powder
- 1 tsp smoked paprika
- 1/2 tsp dried thyme
- 1 tsp Worcestershire sauce
- Salt and pepper to taste

For the breading:

- 50g plain flour
- 100g breadcrumbs
- 2 tbsp grated Parmesan
- 1 egg

Recipe tip:

Make sure you chop those chicken pieces all even-sized so that they cook evenly

Preparation

1. In a large bowl, add chicken pieces, garlic powder, onion powder, paprika, thyme, Worcestershire sauce salt and pepper and mix until combined.

2. In a bowl, add flour, salt, pepper and mix. In another bowl, add eggs and whisk. In a third bowl, add breadcrumbs and Parmesan.

3. Coat each chicken piece with flour, then dip into egg, then coat in breadcrumbs. Shake off any excess breadcrumbs.

4. Add the chicken pieces in a single layer in Zone 1 and Zone 2 drawers, spray with oil (with crisper plate inserted), then insert drawers in unit. Select zone 1, select AIR FRY, set temperature at 190°C for 11 mins, Select MATCH. Press the START/PAUSE button to begin cooking. When time reaches 5 mins, remove drawer, flip **chicken and spray with oil. Reinsert drawer to continue cooking. Serve with your favourite dipping sauce.**

Salt and Pepper Chicken

Serves : 4   *Prep Time : 5 Mins*   *Cook Time : 15 Mins*

Ingredients

- 500g boneless, skinless, chicken breast/thighs, cut into 5-cm pieces
- 1 tbsp oil
- 1/4 tsp garlic powder
- 1 tsp soy sauce
- 1 tsp Chinese 5 spice
- 1 tbsp cornflour
- 1 bell pepper, cut into cubes
- 1 onion, chopped
- Salt and pepper to taste
- Sliced spring onions

Preparation

1. In a bowl, add all ingredients. Mix.

2. Insert crisper plate into Zone 1 drawer. Place the chicken mixture in zone 1 drawer, then insert drawer in unit.

3. Select zone 1, select AIR FRY, set temperature to 190°C, and set time to 15 minutes. Press the START/STOP button to begin cooking. flipping the chicken halfway through cooking time.

4. When cooking is complete, transfer chicken mixture to a plate. Serve with rice topped with sliced spring onions.

Chicken Mains

Chicken Parmesan

Serves : 2   Prep Time : 15 Mins   Cook Time : 18 mins

Ingredients

- 2 tbsp plain flour
- 40g breadcrumbs
- 2 tbsp grated Parmesan
- 1 egg
- 2 skinless chicken breasts
- 4 tbsp pizza topper
- 100g mozzarella slices

Preparation

1. Bash the chicken breasts with a rolling pin until 3-cm in thickness.

2. In a bowl, add flour, salt, pepper and mix. In another bowl, add eggs and whisk. In a third bowl, add breadcrumbs.

3. Coat each chicken breast with flour, then dip into egg, then coat in breadcrumbs.

4. Insert crisper plates into both drawers. Place chicken in Zone 1 and 2 drawers, spray with oil then insert drawers in unit.

5. Select zone 1, select AIR FRY, set temperature to 200°C, and set time to 13 minutes. Select MATCH. Press the START/STOP button to begin cooking.

6. When Zone 1 time reaches 8 minutes, remove drawers from unit and turn the chicken using silicone-tipped tongs. Reinsert drawers to continue cooking.

7. When cooking is complete, remove drawers from unit and top chicken with pizza sauce and mozzarella. Continue to AIR FRY at 200°C for 5 min.
Serve with chips or pasta.

Garlic Chicken Wings and Cheesy Pasta

Serves : 4   Prep Time : 10 Mins   Cook Time : 30 mins

Ingredients

Chicken wings
- 1kg chicken wings
- 2 tbsp cornflour
- 2 tsp smoked paprika
- 2 tsp garlic powder
- Salt and pepper to taste

Cheesy pasta:
- 225g dried spirali pasta
- 120ml double cream
- 600ml whole milk
- 200g mature cheddar cheese, divided
- 2 tbsp butter
- ¼ tsp garlic powder
- ¼ tsp onion powder
- Salt and pepper to taste

Preparation

1. In a bowl, add chicken wings, cornflour, seasoning and mix.

2. Insert a crisper plate into Zone 1 drawer. Place chicken wings in Zone 1 drawer, then insert drawer in unit.

3. With no crisping plate inserted, add all pasta ingredients (except Cheddar) In Zone 2 drawer. Stir. Insert drawer into the unit.

4. Select Zone 1, select AIR FRY, set temperature to 200°C, and set time to 25 minutes. Select Zone 2, select BAKE, set temperature to 170°C and set time for 30 minutes. Select SYNC. Press the START/PAUSE button to begin cooking.

5. Stir the pasta every 10 minutes. and flip the chicken wings halfway cooking time.

6. When cooking is complete, remove drawers from unit, add the Cheddar to the pasta and stir until the cheese is melted. Top the pasta with chicken wings and serve.

Recipe tip:

For golden, crunchy topping:
BAKE at 180°C for 5 minutes, until the cheese is golden brown and bubbly.

Sweet and Spicy Chicken Wings

Serves : 4 | Prep Time : 40 Mins | Cook Time : 20 Mins

Ingredients

- 1 kg chicken wings
- 2 tbsp oil
- Salt and pepper to taste

Tomato and Chilli glaze:

- 2 tbsp Worcestershire sauce
- 150ml tomato ketchup
- 100ml sweet chilli sauce
- 1 tsp chilli flakes
- 2 garlic cloves, minced
- 1 tbsp onion powder
- Salt and pepper to taste

Recipe tip:

- Mix a tablespoon of HP sauce into the glaze for a tangy flavour.
- The spiciness of the glaze can be adjusted by varying the amount of chilli flakes. Start with a smaller amount if you prefer a milder flavour, then add more gradually until you reach the desired level of heat.

Preparation

1. In a bowl, add chicken wings, oil, garlic, salt, pepper and mix. Place the wings in Zone 1 and Zone 2 drawers with crisping plate inserted.

2. Place the wings in Zone 1 and 2 drawers (with crisper plate inserted), then insert drawers in unit. Select Zone, Select AIR FRY, set temperature to 190°C and set time to 15 minutes. Select MATCH. Press START/STOP to begin. Flipping halfway cooking time.

3. In a small saucepan over medium heat, combine all the tomato chilli glaze ingredients. Cook, stirring occasionally, until heated through and combined. Remove from heat.

4. When cooking is complete, remove the wings from the unit and transfer them to a large bowl. Pour the sauce over the chicken wings and mix until evenly coated.

5. Return the wings to the drawers and Air Fry at 200°C for an additional 5 minutes. Serve.

Baked Chicken And Gravy

Serves : 4   Prep Time : 5 Mins   Cook Time : 30 mins

Ingredients

For The Chicken:
- 4 bone in, skin on chicken thighs
- 2 tsp oil
- 1 tsp smoked paprika
- 1 tsp dried thyme
- 1 tsp garlic powder
- Salt & pepper to taste

For The Gravy:
- 4 tbsp plain flour
- 30g butter
- 2 garlic cloves, minced
- 1 onion, finely chopped
- 500ml hot chicken stock
- Salt & pepper to taste

Preparation

1. In a bowl, add chicken, oil, paprika, thyme, garlic powder, salt and pepper. Mix until chicken coated with spices. Set aside.

2. In a bowl, add gravy ingredients and whisk until combined.

3. With no crisping plate installed, Place the chicken into Zone 1 and 2 drawers. Pour the gravy evenly into drawers around the chicken.

4. Select zone 1, select BAKE, set temperature to 190°C, and set time to 30 minutes. Select MATCH. Press the START/STOP button to begin cooking. Flip the thighs and stir the gravy halfway cooking time.

5. When cooking is complete, remove chicken onto a plate, then whisk the gravy until smooth. Serve gravy with chicken.

Chicken Tikka Puff Pies

Serves : 4   Prep Time : 5 Mins   Cook Time : 30 mins

Ingredients

For The Chicken tikka:
- 500g boneless chicken thighs, cut into small pieces
- 80g plain yogurt
- 4 garlic cloves, minced
- 1 tbsp grated ginger
- 1 tsp ground cumin
- 1 tsp garam masala
- 1/2 tsp ground turmeric
- 1 tsp ground coriander
- 1 onion, finely chopped
- 1 tbsp tomato puree
- Salt and pepper to taste

For The Pies:
- 320g ready rolled puff pastry
- 1 egg, whisked (for brushing)

Preparation

1. In a bowl, add all chicken tikka ingredients. Mix until chicken coated with spices. Cover and let it marinate in the fridge for at least 30 minutes.

2. With no crisping plate installed, Place the chicken mixture (including marinade) into Zone 1 drawer.

3. Select zone 1, select AIR FRY, set temperature to 180°C, and set time to 15 minutes. Press the START/STOP button to begin cooking. Stir halfway through cooking time.

4. When cooking is complete, transfer chicken onto a plate. Let cool to room temperature.

5. Cut the pastry sheet into rectangles, depending on the size you prefer. Add spoonfuls of chicken tikka mixture in the center of each pastry square. Fold the pastry over the filling, use a fork to crimp the edges all around. Brush with egg.

6. With crisping plates installed, Place the pies into Zone 1 and Zone 2 drawers. Select zone 1, select BAKE, set temperature to 170°C, and set time to 15 minutes. Select MATCH. Press the START/STOP button to begin cooking. Flip halfway through cooking time.

Recipe tip:

When placing the chicken tikka mixture on the pastry, ensure it's evenly spread and not piled up in the center. This helps in sealing the edges properly and prevents the filling from leaking out during baking.

Chicken Mains

Butter Chicken

Serves : 4   Prep Time : 5 Mins   Cook Time : 35 mins

Ingredients

- 1 kg boneless, skinless chicken thighs, cut into cubes
- 1 (400g) tin chopped tomato
- 20g butter, melted
- 240ml double cream
- 1 large onion, finely chopped
- 3 garlic cloves, minced
- 1 tbsp garam marsala
- 1 tsp ground coriander
- ½ tsp cumin
- 1/4 tsp cinnamon
- 1 tbsp grated fresh ginger
- Salt and pepper to taste

Preparation

1. In a bowl, add all ingredients (except chicken) and whisk until combined. Add the chicken into this mixture and mix until coated with spices.

2. With no crisping plate installed, Place the chicken into Zone 1 drawer. Pour the sauce over the chicken. Insert drawer into the unit.

3. Select Zone 1, select BAKE, set temperature to 180°C, and set time to 35 minutes. Press the START/PAUSE button to begin cooking. When cooking is complete, serve butter chicken with rice.

Recipe tip:

- Serve butter chicken with fluffy basmati rice, or naan bread, or a simple green salad.
- **Leftover butter chicken:** Spread leftover butter chicken sauce on a tortilla, add some cheese, and fold it in half. AIR FRY at 180°C for 7 minutes until golden brown and enjoy a delicious butter chicken quesadilla.

Chicken Mains

Chicken And Dumplings Casserole

Serves : 5 **Prep Time : 15 Mins** **Cook Time : 45 mins**

Ingredients

- 850ml hot chicken stock
- 700g chicken breasts, cut into bite-size pieces
- 1 large onion, finely chopped
- 200g potatoes, peeled and cut into small cubes
- 2 celery stalks, finely chopped
- 3 tbsp tomato puree
- 1 carrot, peeled and thinly sliced
- 1 tsp dried thyme
- 2 tsp plain flour
- Salt & pepper to taste

For the dumplings:
- 170g self-raising flour
- 100g cold butter, cubed
- Pinch of salt
- Cold water, as needed

Preparation

1. In a bowl, whisk together 2 tsp flour and the chicken stock, until combined and smooth. Season with salt and pepper.

2. With no crisping plate installed, add onion, celery, potatoes, carrot, thyme, tomato puree, chicken. Pour over the flour/stock mixture into Zone 1 drawer and stir. Insert drawer in unit.

3. Select Zone 1, select BAKE, set temperature to 180°C, and set time to 45 minutes. Press the START/PAUSE button to begin cooking. When cooking time reaches, 23 minutes, stir.

4. In a bowl, add 170g flour, butter, and salt. Mix until mixture resembles breadcrumbs. Add water gradually while mixing, until dough holds together. Don't over mix. Divide into 8 balls.

5. When time reaches 30 minutes, remove drawer stir and place dumplings on top of chicken. Reinsert drawer to continue cooking. When cooking is complete, serve.

Chicken Fajitas Bowls

Serves : 4   Prep Time : 5 Mins   Cook Time : 15 mins

Ingredients

Chicken Fajitas:
- Juice of one lemon
- 2 tbsp oil
- 500g boneless, skinless chicken thighs or breasts, cut into strips
- 1 tsp garlic powder
- 1 tsp onion powder
- 1 tsp smoked paprika
- ½ tsp ground cumin
- 1 medium onion, sliced
- 1 red bell pepper, sliced
- 1 garlic clove, minced

For the rice:
- 1 pouch (250g) microwave long grain rice, uncooked
- 50ml chicken stock
- 1 tbsp tomato puree
- Salt and pepper to taste

Preparation

1. In a bowl, add Chicken Fajitas ingredients and mix until all coated with seasoning and oil.

2. Install a crisping plate in the Zone 1 drawer, then chicken/pepper mixture in the drawer and insert drawer in unit.

3. With no crisping plate installed, place rice, stock, tomato puree, salt and pepper in the Zone 2 drawer and stir.

4. Select Zone 1, select AIR FRY, set temperature to 190°C, and set time to 15 minutes. Select Zone 2, select BAKE, set temperature to 190°C and set time for 10 minutes. Select SYNC. Press the START/PAUSE button to begin cooking.

5. When the Zone 1 time reaches 10 minutes, remove drawers from unit and stir chicken. Reinsert drawer to continue cooking. When cooking is complete, mix chicken fajitas **with rice and serve.**

Fish Mains

Lemon and Butter Salmon

Serves : 4   **Prep Time : 5 Mins**   **Cook Time : 10 mins**

Ingredients

- 4 salmon fillets, room temperature
- 2 garlic cloves, minced
- Juice and zest of 1 lemon
- 5 springs fresh rosemary, roughly chopped
- Salt and pepper to taste
- 2 tbsp butter, melted

Recipe Variation:

- **Garlic Parmesan Crusted Salmon:** Mix 50g grated Parmesan, 1 tsp dried oregano and 1 tsp minced garlic into softened butter. Spread this mixture over the salmon fillets before air frying.
- **Honey Mustard Glazed Salmon:** Mix 2 tsp honey, 3 tbsp English mustard, 1 tsp lemon juice, season with salt, pepper, 1/2 tsp smoked paprika and brush over the salmon before air frying.
- **Teriyaki-style Glazed Salmon:** Mix 60ml soy sauce, 1 tbsp brown sugar, 1 tsp fresh grated ginger, and 1 minced garlic clove and brush over the salmon before air frying.
- If you have more time, marinate the salmon in the glaze for 15-30 minutes before cooking. This allows the flavours to infuse into the salmon.

Preparation

1. In a bowl, add all ingredients and mix until salmon coated with spices.

2. Insert a crisper plate into Zone 1 drawer. Place salmon in drawer, then insert drawer in unit. Pour any remaining seasoning over the salmon.

3. Select zone 1, select AIR FRY, set temperature to 200°C, and set time to 9-10 minutes (depending on the salmon thickness, the salmon is cooked when its internal temperature reaches 63°C). Press the START/STOP button to begin cooking. Serve with an extra squeeze of lemon.

Fish Mains

Kedgeree

Serves : 4   Prep Time : 5 Mins   Cook Time : 15 Mins

Ingredients

- 2 pouch (250g each) microwave long grain rice, uncooked
- 20g butter
- 1 tsp onion powder
- 1/2 tsp garlic powder
- 1 tbsp curry powder
- 1/2 tsp turmeric powder
- 250g smoked haddock, poached in boiling water for 5 mins
- 120ml chicken stock
- 4 large eggs
- Salt & pepper to taste

Preparation

1. With no crisping plate installed, place rice, stock, butter, onion powder, garlic powder, curry powder, salt and pepper in the Zone 1 drawer and stir to combine. Insert drawer in unit.

2. Insert the crisper plates in Zone 2 drawer. Place eggs on crisper plate. Insert drawer in unit.

3. Select Zone 1, select BAKE, set temperature to 190°C and set time for 12 minutes. Select Zone 2, select AIR FRY, set temperature to 150°C, and set time to 15 minutes. Select SYNC. Press the START/PAUSE button to begin cooking. When cooking time in Zone 1 reaches 6 minutes, stir the rice and reinsert drawer to continue cooking.

4. When cooking is complete, remove eggs and place in a bowl of iced water for a minute, Peel the eggs and cut in quarters. Flake the fish, then add it to rice and stir until gently heated through. Serve with eggs.

Fish Mains

Fish Fingers and Mushy Peas

Serves : 4   **Prep Time : 10 Mins**   **Cook Time : 14 mins**

Ingredients

- 450g cod, haddock or any white fillets, thawed
- 5 tbsp plain flour
- 1 tbsp smoked paprika
- Zest of 1 small lemon
- 70g breadcrumbs
- 2 large eggs

For the Mushy Peas:

- 500g frozen garden peas
- 2 tsp butter
- Zest of 1 small lemon
- 100ml boiling water
- Salt and pepper to taste

Recipe tip:

For an extra crispy coating, you can double bread the fish fingers. After dipping them in the egg mixture and breadcrumbs once, dip them back into the egg mixture and breadcrumbs again.

Preparation

1. In a shallow bowl add flour and season with salt and pepper, in another bowl add the egg, whisk, and add breadcrumbs in a third shallow bowl.

2. Slice the fish fillets lengthways into 3-cm wide fingers. Coat fish with flour, then in the beaten egg, and finally in breadcrumbs, pressing to coat.

3. Insert a crisper plate into Zone 1 drawer. Place fish fingers in Zone 1 drawer, brush with oil, then insert drawer in unit.

4. With no crisping plate installed, add peas, butter, water, salt, and pepper to Zone 2 drawer. Stir to combine. Insert drawer into the unit.

5. Select zone 1, select AIR FRY, set temperature to 190°C, and set time to 12 minutes. Select zone 2, select BAKE, set temperature to 180°C, and set time to 13 minutes. Select SYNC. Press the START/STOP button to begin cooking.

6. When Zone 1 and 2 time reaches 6 minutes, remove drawers from unit, flip the fish fingers using silicone-tipped tongs and stir the peas. Reinsert drawers to continue cooking.

7. When cooking is complete, remove drawers from unit and mash the peas with a fork. Serve fish fingers with mushy peas.

Fish Mains

Sweet Chilli Salmon with Egg Noodles

🛎 Serves : 4   🧂 Prep Time : 5 Mins   ⬛ Cook Time : 10 Mins

Ingredients

For the egg noodles:
- 300g egg noodles (Fresh noodles)
- 1 tbsp oil
- 1/2 tsp grated fresh ginger
- 2 garlic cloves, minced
- 100ml vegetable stock or water
- 2 tbsp light soy sauce
- 1 tbsp dark soy sauce
- 150g frozen peas
- 1 small bell pepper, finely chopped
- 1 tsp dark brown sugar
- Pinch of chilli flakes (optional)
- Pepper to taste

For the salmon:
- 4 salmon fillets (170g each)
- 1 tsp oil
- 1 garlic clove, minced
- 1 tbsp sweet chilli sauce
- 1 tsp chopped fresh or dried dill
- Juice of 1 lemon
- pinch of chilli flakes (optional)
- Salt and pepper to taste

Preparation

1. Add oil, garlic, dill, sweet chilli sauce, lemon juice, chilli flakes, salt and pepper in a bowl and mix. add the salmon fillets and coat with the marinade. Set aside for 5 minutes.

2. Place all egg noodle ingredients in Zone 1 drawer and stir (With no crisping plate inserted).
Insert crisping plate in Zone 2 drawer. Place the salmon fillets in the drawer.

3. Select zone 1, select AIR FRY, set temperature to 190°C, and set time to 10 minutes. Select zone 2, select AIR FRY, set temperature to 200°C, and set time to 9-10 minutes. Select SYNC. Press the START/STOP button to begin cooking.

4. Flip the salmon and stir the noodles halfway cooking time.

5. when cooking is complete, remove the salmon from the unit. Stir the noodle. and serve the noddle topped with salmon.

Sweet Chilli Salmon with Egg Noodles

With the tasty combination of salmon, and the sweet, spicy noodles, this dish is sure to be a winner.

Fish Mains

Salmon and Dill Parcels

Serves : 4 **Prep Time : 5 Mins** **Cook Time : 20 mins**

Ingredients

- 320g ready rolled puff pastry
- 1 egg, whisked (for brushing)

For the salmon:
- 4 boneless and skinless salmon fillets, (170g each)
- 4 tbsp chopped fresh dill
- Salt and pepper to taste

For the cream cheese sauce:
- 150g soft cream cheese
- ½ tsp dried thyme
- 1 tsp onion powder
- ½ tsp garlic powder
- ½ tsp English Mustard
- Salt and pepper to taste

Recipe Variation:

- Sauté fresh spinach with 2 minced garlic cloves and 1 tsp butter until wilted, then place it on top of the salmon and cheese sauce before wrapping in pastry, it'll add a lovely bit of green and some extra flavour.

Preparation

1. In a bowl, add all cream cheese sauce and mix until combined.

2. Pat the salmon fillets dry and season with salt and pepper.

3. Cut the pastry sheet into rectangles, depending on the size of salmon fillets. Place a salmon fillet in the center of each pastry rectangle. Sprinkle chopped dill over the salmon and add spoonfuls of cream cheese sauce over the salmon and dill.

4. Fold the pastry over the salmon, use a fork to crimp the edges all around. Brush with egg.

5. With crisping plates installed, Place the Parcels into Zone 1 and Zone 2 drawers. Select zone 1, select BAKE, set temperature to 160°C, and set time to 16-20 minutes (depending on the salmon thickness, the salmon is cooked when its internal temperature reaches 63°C). Select MATCH. Press the START/STOP button to begin cooking. Flip halfway through cooking time.

6. Remove from unit and let the parcels cool for a few minutes before serving.

Salmon and Dill Parcels

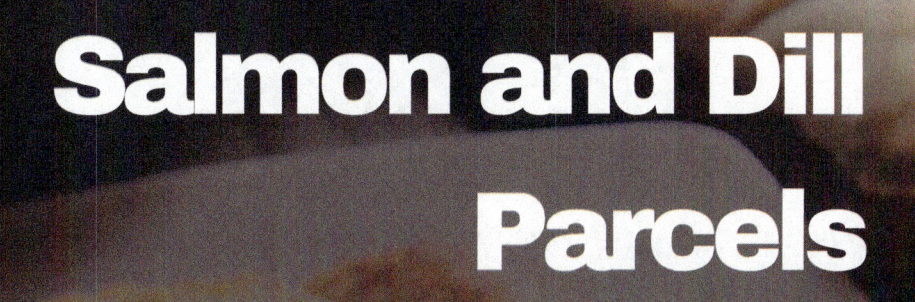

A golden, flaky crust enveloping tender salmon, fragrant dill, and creamy sauce that will surely impress your taste buds. These little beauties are a guaranteed crowd-pleaser, perfect for elevating any dinner party from ordinary to absolutely brilliant!

Fish Mains

Fish Cakes

Serves : 4   **Prep Time : 10 Mins**   **Cook Time : 13 mins**

Ingredients

- 350g cod or white fish fillets
- 70g breadcrumbs
- 2 tbsp finely chopped fresh coriander
- 1 garlic clove, minced
- 2 tbsp mayonnaise
- 1 egg
- Salt and pepper to taste

For the Breading:

- 70g breadcrumbs
- 1 large egg, whisked

Preparation

1. In a food processor add all ingredients and pulse a few times until crumbly. Shape mixture into 4 fish cakes. Coat the fish cakes with egg, and finally in breadcrumbs, pressing to coat.

2. Insert a crisper plate into both drawers. Brush plates with oil. Place fish cakes in Zone 1 and 2 drawers, spray/drizzle with oil, then insert drawers in unit.

3. Select zone 1, select AIR FRY, set temperature to 190°C, and set time to 13 minutes. Select MATCH. Press the START/STOP button to begin cooking.

4. When Zone 1 reaches 7 minutes, remove drawers from unit and flip the fish cakes using silicone-tipped tongs. Reinsert drawers to continue cooking.

5. When cooking is complete, remove drawers from unit and serve fish cakes with lemon wedges.

Fish Mains

Tuna Pasta Bake

Serves : 4 **Prep Time : 5 Mins** **Cook Time : 35 mins**

Ingredients

- 200g dry fusilli pasta
- 1 tbsp butter
- 1 tbsp oil
- 1 onion, finely chopped
- 2 garlic cloves, minced
- 1 (400g) tin chopped tomatoes
- 300ml water
- 200g tinned tuna in oil, drained
- 80g grated mature cheddar
- Salt and pepper to taste

Preparation

1. With no crisping plate installed, add butter, oil, garlic, onion, tuna, pasta, tomatoes, salt, and pepper to Zone 1 and 2 drawers (divide the amount between the two drawers). Stir to combine. Cover with tin. Insert drawers into the unit.

2. Select zone 1, select BAKE, set temperature to 170°C, and set time to 35 minutes. Select MATCH. Press the START/STOP button to begin cooking. Stir the pasta every 10 minutes.

3. When the time reaches 30 minutes, remove the drawers from the device, stir and sprinkle with grated cheese. Insert drawers into the unit to continue cooking.
   When cooking is complete, remove from unit, and serve

Garlic Butter Prawns

Serves : 4   Prep Time : 5 Mins   Cook Time : 13 mins

Ingredients

- 600g prawns, peeled and deveined
- 60ml melted butter
- 3 garlic cloves, minced
- Juice of 1 medium lemon
- Salt and pepper to taste

Recipe Variation:

- **Honey Garlic Prawns: :** Combine 1 tbsp honey, 2 tbsp soy sauce, 3 minced garlic, and a splash of vinegar. Toss the prawns in the sauce.

Preparation

1. With no crisping plate installed, add butter, garlic, prawns, lemon juice, salt, and pepper to Zone 1 drawer. Stir to combine. Insert drawer into the unit.

2. Select zone 1, select BAKE, set temperature to 200°C, and set time to 13 minutes. Press the START/STOP button to begin cooking.

3. When time reaches 8 minutes in zone 1 drawer. Remove drawer and stir. Reinsert drawer in unit to continue cooking.
   When cooking is complete, serve prawns with garlic butter sauce.

Fish Mains

Prawns and Broccoli with Herbed Rice

Serves : 4   Prep Time : 10 Mins   Cook Time : 15 mins

Ingredients

Prawns and broccoli:
- 500g prawns, peeled and deveined
- 200g frozen broccoli florets, thawed
- 2 tbsp cornflour
- 2 tsp soy sauce
- 5 tbsp chicken stock
- 4 garlic cloves, minced
- 1 tsp white vinegar
- 1 tsp grated fresh ginger
- Salt and pepper to taste

Herbed rice:
- 120ml vegetable stock
- 2 pouch (250g) microwave long grain rice, uncooked
- 2 tbsp butter
- 1/2 tbsp parsley, finely chopped
- 1 tbsp tomato puree
- 1 tsp curry powder
- 1/4 tbsp dried thyme
- Salt and pepper to taste

Preparation

1. With no crisping plate installed, place all Prawns and broccoli ingredients in Zone 1 drawer, mix until broccoli and prawns coated with seasoning then insert drawer in unit.

2. With no crisping plate installed, add all rice ingredients in Zone 2 drawer. Stir. Insert drawer into the unit.

3. Select Zone 1, select AIR FRY, set temperature to 200°C, and set time to 15 minutes. Select Zone 2, select BAKE, set temperature to 200°C and set time for 12 minutes. Select SYNC. Press the START/PAUSE button to begin cooking. Stir the prawns and rice halfway cooking time.
When cooking is complete, remove drawers from unit. Fluff the rice with a fork and serve with prawns and broccoli.

Fish Mains

Breaded Cod Loins with Herb Butter Potatoes

Serves : 4 **Prep Time : 5 Mins** **Cook Time : 25 Mins**

Ingredients

- 4 cod loins, patted dry with kitchen paper
- 40g plain flour
- 1/4 tsp garlic powder
- 1/2 tsp smoked paprika
- 30g grated Parmesan
- 150g breadcrumbs
- 1 large egg
- Salt and pepper to taste

Herb butter potatoes:

- 50g butter, softened
- 500g baby potatoes, halved if large
- 1 tbsp oil
- 1 tsp finely chopped fresh rosemary
- 2 garlic cloves, minced
- Salt and pepper to taste

Preparation

1. In a bowl, add potatoes, and oil. Mix.

2. In a bowl, whisk the eggs. In a second bowl, add the flour and season with paprika, garlic powder salt and pepper. In a third bowl, add the breadcrumbs and parmesan.
Dip each piece of cod first in the flour, then in the egg, then finally the breadcrumbs.

3. Insert a crisper plate into Zone 1 drawer. Place the cod in Zone 1 drawer, spray/drizzle with oil. With no crisping plate installed, add potatoes to Zone 2 drawer. Insert drawers into the unit.

4. Select zone 1, select AIR FRY, set temperature to 180°C, and set time to 12 minutes. Select zone 1, select AIR FRY, set temperature to 200°C, and set time to 25 minutes. Select SYNC. Press the START/STOP button to begin cooking.

5. When Zone 1 time reaches 6 minutes, remove drawers from unit, flip the cod. Reinsert drawer to continue cooking.

6. When cooking is complete, use tongs to remove fish from the tray. Add butter, rosemary, garlic, salt and pepper to the potatoes and stir. AIR FRY at 200°C, for 5 minutes. Serve the potatoes with the cod.

Recipe tip:

Flip the potatoes every 5 minutes to ensure even cooking

84

Afternoon Tea

You're going to love these British afternoon tea ideas!

Afternoon Tea

Hot Cross Buns

Serves : 8   **Prep Time : 2 Hours**   **Cook Time : 20 mins**

Ingredients

- 450g plain flour, divided
- 100g caster sugar, divided
- 70g butter
- Pinch of salt
- 180ml milk, warm
- 2 1/4 tsp dried yeast
- 2 large egg, beaten
- 1/2 tsp ground cinnamon
- 1/2 tsp ground nutmeg
- 150g sultanas

For the cross
- 70g plain flour mixed with 140ml water

For brushing
- Golden syrup

Preparation

1. In a bowl, add milk, yeast, and 2 tsp of caster sugar. Cover and sit for about 6 minutes.

2. After the 6 minutes, add remaining sugar, butter, eggs, salt, cinnamon, nutmeg, allspice, and 125g of the flour to the milk mixture. Mix with wooden spoon for 30 seconds.

3. Add the remaining flour and sultanas. Continue to knead for 3 more minutes. Dough will be a little sticky and soft. (If the dough is too sticky add more flour 1 tbsp at a time).

4. Leave the dough in the bowl and cover and let it rise in a warm place for about 1 hour until doubled in size.

5. Punch the dough down to release the air. Divide dough into 8 pieces. Roll them into 8 balls.

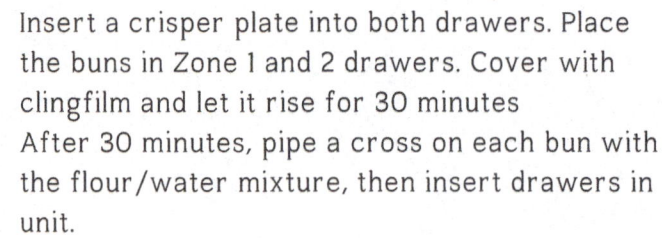

6. Insert a crisper plate into both drawers. Place the buns in Zone 1 and 2 drawers. Cover with clingfilm and let it rise for 30 minutes
After 30 minutes, pipe a cross on each bun with the flour/water mixture, then insert drawers in unit.

7. Select zone 1, select BAKE, set temperature to 160°C, and set time to 18-20 minutes. Select MATCH. Press the START/STOP button to begin cooking.

8. When cooking is complete, remove from unit and allow to cool for a few minutes, then brush with golden syrup or apricot jam. Serve.

Cheese Scones

🔔 Serves : 5   🥣 Prep Time : 10 Mins   🍞 Cook Time : 13 mins

Ingredients

- 200g self-raising flour
- ¼ tsp mustard powder
- ½ tsp baking powder
- 100g cold butter, cut into cubes
- 120g grated mature cheddar
- Pinch of salt
- Cold Milk, as needed

Recipe Variation:

- **Fruit Scones:** Add dried fruit such as sultanas, or currants.
- **Lemon Drizzle-inspired Scones**: Add lemon zest into the dough and drizzle them with a lemon glaze made from icing sugar and lemon juice after baking.
- **Cherry Bakewell Scones:** Add chopped glacé cherries and chopped almonds in the dough, top with a layer of almond-flavoured icing and a cherry on top.

Preparation

1. In a bowl, add flour, salt, baking powder, mustard powder. Mix until combined. Add the butter, rub the butter into the flour mixture until it resembles coarse crumbs. Add the cheese and stir with spoon. Add milk gradually while mixing until a dough comes together (Do Not over mix).

2. Transfer the dough to a lightly floured surface, and lightly roll into 3-cm in thickness. Cut out 5-cm scones. Brush with milk.

3. Insert crisper plates into both drawers. Place the scones in Zone 1 and 2 drawers, then insert drawers in unit.

4. Select zone 1, select BAKE, set temperature to 170°C, and set time to 13 minutes. Select MATCH. Press the START/STOP button to begin cooking.

5. When cooking is complete, remove from unit and serve warm.

Afternoon Tea

Madeira Cake

Serves : 4-6 **Prep Time : 10 Mins** **Cook Time : 40 mins**

Ingredients

- 270g butter, softened
- 270g caster sugar
- Zest of 1 lemon
- 3 large eggs, room temperature
- 3 tbsp milk
- 270g plain flour
- 2 tsp baking powder

Recipe Variation:

- **Coffee and Walnut Madeira Cake:** Add 2 tbsp instant coffee granules, dissolved in 2 tbsp hot water to the batter and fold in 100g chopped walnuts into the batter.
- **Marbled Madeira Cake:** Divide the cake batter in half and stir (2 tbsp cocoa powder mixed with 3 tbsp milk) into one half. Alternate spoonfuls of the plain and chocolate batters in the cake tin and use a skewer to create a marbled effect before baking.
- **Lemon Drizzle Cake:** Add zest of 1 large lemon to the batter and after baking drizzle with a lemon drizzle (For the lemon drizzle mix 200g icing sugar with 1 tbsp lemon juice until a sightly thick paste formed).

Preparation

1. In a bowl, add butter and sugar. Whisk until creamy, add lemon zest and eggs one at a time while whisking. Add the flour and baking powder to the butter mixture gradually while whisking until combined.

2. Grease two 1-lb loaf cake tins. Pour the cake batter into the tins. Install crisping plates in Zone 1 and 2 drawers, place tins in drawers, insert drawers in unit.

3. Select Zone 1, select Bake, set temperature to 150°C, and set time to 40 minutes. Select MATCH. Press the START/PAUSE button to begin cooking.

4. When cooking is complete, cool in tins for 5 minutes before removing to a wire rack to cool completely. Slice and serve.

Bakewell Tart

Serves : 4-6   Prep Time : 1 Hour   Cook Time : 35 mins

Ingredients

For the pastry crust:
- 250g plain flour
- Pinch of salt
- 40g icing sugar
- 170g butter, frozen and grated
- 1 large egg yolk
- Ice cold water

For the filling:
- 250g butter, soft
- 200g caster sugar
- 1 ½ tsp almond extract
- 2 large eggs
- 250g almond flour
- Pinch of salt
- 30g plain flour
- 120g raspberry conserve
- 50g almond slices

Preparation

1. In a large bowl, add flour, salt, icing sugar. Mix until combined. Add the butter, and mix until it forms a coarse breadcrumbs. Add egg yolk, and water gradually and mix just until the dough comes together.

2. Divide the dough into 2 equal portions. Wrap in cling film and refrigerate for 30 minutes.

3. On a lightly floured surface, roll each dough large enough to line the base and sides of a 14-cm tart tin.

4. Gently press the dough into the sides of the tart tin. Prick the bottom with a fork and freeze for 30 minutes.

5. Line the pies with tin foil and fill with the with baking beans. Insert crisper plates into both drawers. Place the tins in Zone 1 and 2 drawers, then insert drawers in unit.

6. Select zone 1, select BAKE, set temperature to 180°C, and set time to 15 minutes. Select MATCH. Press the START/STOP button to begin cooking.

7. When time reaches 10 minutes in Zone 1 and 2 drawers, remove drawers from unit, remove the foil and baking beans. Reinsert drawers to continue cooking.

8. In a large bowl, add all filling ingredients (except almond slices) and whisk until combined and smooth.

9. When cooking is complete, remove the tins from the drawers and spread each tart base with raspberry conserve and divide the filling mixture evenly between the two tarts , smooth the surface. Sprinkle with almond slices.

10. Place the tins in Zone 1 and 2 drawers, then insert drawers in unit. Select zone 1, select BAKE, set temperature to 165°C, and set time to 20 minutes. Select MATCH. Press the START/STOP button to begin cooking.

11. When cooking is complete, remove from unit and cool completely before serving.

Afternoon Tea

Apple Crumble Cake

Serves : 8   Prep Time : 10 Mins   Cook Time : 18 mins

Ingredients

For the Crumble Topping:
- 60g butter, melted
- 90g plain flour
- 60g caster sugar
- ¼ tsp ground cinnamon

For the Apple Cake:
- 240g plain flour
- 2 tsp baking powder
- 1 tsp ground cinnamon
- 115g butter, softened
- 150g caster sugar
- 3 medium eggs, room temperature
- 1 ½ tsp vanilla extract
- 80ml milk
- 3 Granny Smith apples peeled, thinly sliced and lightly coated with flour
- Pinch of salt
- Pinch of nutmeg

Preparation

1. In a bowl, add topping ingredients and mix until combined and crumbly.

2. In a bowl, add butter and sugar. Whisk until creamy, add vanilla, milk and eggs one at a time while beating. Add the flour and baking powder to the butter mixture gradually while whisking until combined. Fold in the apples.

3. Grease 8 individual muffin tins. Pour the cake batter into the muffin tins. Insert crisper plates into both drawers. Place the tins into Zone 1 and 2 drawers. Insert drawers in unit.

4. Select zone 1, select BAKE, set temperature to 160°C and set time to 18 minutes. Press the START/STOP button to begin cooking.

5. When cooking is complete, check the cakes are ready by inserting a skewer into the centre. If it comes out clean, remove the cakes from drawers and cool completely on a wire rack. If not, bake for another 3 minutes. Serve.

Afternoon Tea

Mini Victoria Sponge Cakes

Serves : 6   **Prep Time : 15 Mins**   **Cook Time : 13 mins**

Ingredients

Cake :
- 120g butter, softened
- 120g caster sugar
- 2 medium eggs
- 120g self-raising flour
- 1 tsp baking powder
- 1 tbsp milk
- 1 tsp vanilla extract

Filling:
- 300ml double cream, whipped
- 4 tbsp raspberry/blueberry conserve

Preparation

1. In a bowl, add butter and sugar. Whisk until creamy, add vanilla and eggs one at a time while whisking. Add the flour and baking powder to the butter mixture gradually while whisking until combined.

2. Grease individual cake tins, pour the cake batter into the greased tins.

3. Insert crisper plates into both drawers. Place the cake tins in Zone 1 and 2 drawers, then insert drawers in unit.

4. Select zone 1, select BAKE, set temperature to 160°C, and set time to 13 minutes. Select MATCH. Press the START/STOP button to begin cooking.

5. When cooking is complete, check the cakes are ready by inserting a skewer into the centre. If it comes out clean, remove the cakes from drawers and cool completely on a wire rack. If not, bake for another 3 minutes before testing again with a skewer.
When ready to serve, slice each cake in half fill with double cream and raspberry/blueberry conserve.

Welsh Cakes

Serves : 4   **Prep Time : 15 Mins**   **Cook Time : 13 mins**

Ingredients

- 110g self-raising flour
- 55g cold butter, cubed
- Pinch of salt
- 1/4 tsp mixed spice
- 30g caster sugar
- 1 handful of sultanas
- 1 large egg
- A few drops of milk, if needed
- 2 tbsp melted butter, for brushing

Preparation

1. In a bowl, add flour, mixed spice, salt and butter. Rub mixture using hands until resembles breadcrumbs. Stir in the sugar and the sultanas. Add the egg. Mix to a firm dough (if it is too dry, add some drops of milk gradually).

2. Transfer to a floured surface, roll out to 1 1/2-cm thickness, then cut into circles.

3. Insert crisper plates into both drawers. Place the welsh cakes in Zone 1 and 2 drawers, brush with some melted butter, then insert drawers in unit.

4. Select zone 1, select BAKE, set temperature to 170°C, and set time to 13 minutes. Select MATCH. Press the START/STOP button to begin cooking.

5. When time reaches 5 minutes, remove drawers from unit. Flip the welsh cakes and reinsert drawers to continue cooking.
When cooking is complete, remove from unit and serve warm.

Custard Creams

Makes : 24 Custard Creams **Prep Time : 15 Mins** **Cook Time : 13 mins**

Ingredients

- 220g plain flour
- 220g butter, softened
- 80g icing sugar
- 100g No added sugar custard powder

For the filling:

- 100g butter, softened
- 250g icing sugar
- 1 lemon zest
- 1 tbsp lemon juice

Preparation

1. In a bowl, add the butter and whisk until creamy, then whisk in the icing sugar, then mix in the other ingredients until combined and form a dough.

2. Transfer dough to a work surface and roll it into a log and cut into 48 equal portions. Roll each portion into a ball and flatten with a fork slightly.

3. Insert crisper plates into both drawers. Place the Custard Creams 3-cm apart in Zone 1 and 2 drawers, then insert drawers in unit.

4. Select zone 1, select BAKE, set temperature to 160°C, and set time to 13 minutes. Select MATCH. Press the START/STOP button to begin cooking. When cooking is complete, remove from unit and set aside for 30 minutes to cool.

5. In a bowl, add the filling ingredients and whisk until light and creamy. Spread the icing on each biscuit half (24 half) and sandwich together with remaining biscuits.

Afternoon Tea

Bara Brith

Makes 10 large slices Prep Time : 15 Mins Cook Time : 50 mins

Ingredients

- 400g mixed dried fruit, soaked overnight in 300ml hot black tea and 150g brown sugar
- 130g butter, softened
- 250g self-raising flour
- 1 tsp mixed spice
- 1 egg, whisked

Preparation

1. Add flour, butter, mixed spice and egg into the bowl of soaked mixed fruit. Mix until combined.

2. Grease and two 1-lb loaf tins with baking paper. Pour the mixture evenly into loaf tins.

3. With no crisping plates installed. Place loaf tins into Zone 1 and 2 drawers. Insert drawers in unit.

4. Select zone 1, select BAKE, set temperature to 150°C, and set time to 50 minutes. Select MATCH. Press the START/STOP button to begin cooking.

5. When cooking is complete, remove from unit and and allow it to cool in the tin for 10 minutes. Then, transfer it to a wire rack to cool completely. Once cooled, slice and serve with butter, if desired.

Afternoon Tea

Sticky Toffee Pudding

Makes 6 puddings   **Prep Time : 10 Mins**   **Cook Time : 20 mins**

Ingredients

- 4 tbsp golden syrup
- 70g soft butter
- 80g brown sugar
- 2 medium eggs
- 190g self-raising flour
- 1/2 tsp baking powder
- 150g dates, pitted, chopped and soaked in 200ml boiling water for 30 minutes
- 2 tbsp milk

Preparation

1. Grease six 180ml/4oz ramekins. Mash the soaked dates with a fork.

2. In a bowl, add butter, golden syrup and sugar, mix using a hand mixer until creamy. Add flour, baking powder, and eggs. mix with spoon until combined. Add mashed dates and milk. Mix with spoon until combined. Fill the ramekins 2/3 way up with the pudding.

3. With crisping plates installed. Place ramekins into Zone 1 and 2 drawers. Insert drawers in unit.

4. Select zone 1, select BAKE, set temperature to 160°C, and set time to 20 minutes. Select MATCH. Press the START/STOP button to begin cooking (use a skewer to check the pudding. If it comes out clean, the pudding is ready. If not, bake for a further 5 minutes covered with foil).

5. When cooking is complete, remove from unit and turn upside down on serving plate. Serve warm.

6. **For the butterscotch sauce:**
On a pan over medium heat, add 50g butter, 150g brown sugar, 300ml double cream. Stir and bring to a boil. Simmer for 2 minutes, then remove from heat. Serve warm with the sticky toffee pudding.

Afternoon Tea

Hobnob Biscuits

Makes : 20 biscuits **Prep Time : 15 Mins** **Cook Time : 25 mins**

Ingredients

- 150g self-raising flour
- 100g caster sugar
- 150g soft butter
- 1 tbsp milk
- 2 tbsp golden syrup
- 1/2 tsp bicarbonate of soda
- 120g jumbo oats

Preparation

1. In a large bowl, add sugar and butter. Beat with a mixer until light and creamy. Add the milk, golden syrup, and beat.

2. Add the flour and bicarbonate of soda into the butter mixture and mix using a spoon. Add the oats and mix. Refrigerate for 10 minutes.

3. Divide the dough into 25g spoonfuls. Quickly roll into balls.

4. With crisping plates installed. Place biscuits into Zone 1 and 2 drawers. Insert drawers in unit.

5. Select zone 1, select BAKE, set temperature to 140°C, and set time to 25 minutes. Select MATCH. Press the START/STOP button to begin cooking .

6. When cooking is complete, remove from unit and let set for 10 min. Transfer Biscuits to a cooling rack until completely cool.

Afternoon Tea

Ginger Biscuits

Makes : 20 biscuits **Prep Time : 15 Mins** **Cook Time : 11 mins**

Ingredients

- 150g plain flour
- 100g soft butter
- 100g brown sugar
- 2 tbsp golden syrup
- 1 medium egg
- 1 tsp ground ginger
- 1 tsp ground cinnamon
- 1/2 tsp bicarbonate of soda
- Pinch of salt

Recipe Variation:

For added flavour, you can mix in some finely chopped Crystallised ginger or ground nutmeg with the dry ingredients. OR Fold in chopped nuts like almonds, pecans, or walnuts for added crunch.

Preparation

1. In a bowl, add flour, ginger, cinnamon, salt, and bicarbonate of soda. Mix and set aside.

2. In another bowl, whisk the soft butter and sugar until light and fluffy. Add the egg, golden syrup and whisk until combined. Add the flour mixture into the butter mixture and mix until a dough forms.

3. Roll the dough into 2-cm thickness, cut out circles. Place the circles in the zone 1 and 2 drawers, spaced apart (with crisping plates installed). Insert drawers in unit.

4. Select zone 1, select BAKE, set temperature to 170°C, and set time to 11 minutes. Select MATCH. Press the START/STOP button to begin cooking.

5. When cooking is complete, remove from unit and let set for 10 min. Transfer Biscuits to a cooling rack until completely cool.

Carrot Cake Loaf

Serves: 6 | Prep Time : 10 Mins | Cook Time : 40 mins

Ingredients

Carrot Cake:
- 150g brown sugar
- 150ml vegetable oil
- 100g grated carrots
- 100g walnuts, finely chopped
- 2 large eggs
- 150g plain flour
- 1 tsp bicarbonate of soda
- 1 tsp baking powder
- ½ tsp cinnamon
- 1/4 tsp ground nutmeg
- Pinch of salt

Icing:
- 115g cream cheese, room temperature
- 2 tbsp butter
- 200g icing sugar

Preparation

1. In a large bowl, add flour, baking powder, bicarbonate of soda, cinnamon, nutmeg, salt. Mix and set aside.

2. In another bowl, add eggs, sugar and oil. Beat with a hand mixer until combined.

3. Pour the egg mixture into the flour mixture. Mix until combined. Add the grated carrots, walnuts and mix with a wooden spoon until combined.

4. Grease two 1-lb loaf tins and pour the batter into the greased tins.

5. With no crisping plates installed. Place the tins into Zone 1 and 2 drawers. Insert drawer in unit.

6. Select zone 1, select BAKE, set temperature to 150°C, and set time to 40 minutes. Select MATCH. Press the START/STOP button to begin cooking (use a skewer to check the cake. If it comes out clean, the cake is ready. If not, bake for a further 5 minutes covering with tin foil).

7. When cooking is complete, remove from unit and let cool completely.

8. In a bowl, add all icing ingredients and beat with hand mixer (or with a whisk) until smooth. Do Not over mix the icing. Spread the icing on top of the cake sprinkle with walnuts. Slice, serve.

Afternoon Tea

Chocolate Chip Butternut Squash Cake

Serves: 6   **Prep Time : 10 Mins**   **Cook Time : 40 mins**

Ingredients

- 200g brown sugar
- 180ml vegetable oil
- 200g butternut squash puree
- 3 large eggs
- 250g plain flour
- 1 tsp bicarbonate of soda
- 2 tsp baking powder
- ½ tsp cinnamon
- 2 tsp vanilla extract
- Pinch of salt
- 100g chocolate chips

Recipe tip:

For the pumpkin puree, simply roast or boil a Butternut Squash Chunks until tender, drain well (if boiled) then blend until smooth.

Preparation

1. In a bowl, add flour, bicarbonate of soda, baking powder, salt, cinnamon, nutmeg, and ginger. Mix until combined. Set aside.

2. In another bowl, add pumpkin puree, sugar, brown sugar, melted butter, eggs, and vanilla. Whisk until combined.

3. Pour the pumpkin mixture into the flour mixture. Mix until combined. Add chocolate chips and stir with a spoon until combined.

4. Grease two 1-lb loaf tins and pour the batter into the tins.

5. With no crisping plates installed. Place the tins into Zone 1 and 2 drawers. Insert drawer in unit.

6. Select zone 1, select BAKE, set temperature to 150°C, and set time to 40 minutes. Select MATCH. Press the START/STOP button to begin cooking (use a skewer to check the cake. If it comes out clean, the cake is ready. If not, bake for a further 5 minutes covering with tin foil).

7. When cooking is complete, remove from unit and let cool completely. Once cooled, slice the chocolate chip pumpkin cake loaf and serve. Enjoy with a cup tea.

100

Afternoon Tea

Yorkshire Parkin

Serves: 16 **Prep Time : 15 Mins** **Cook Time : 50 Mins**

Ingredients

- 200g porridge oats
- 200g plain flour
- 1 1/2 tsp baking powder
- 2 tsp ground ginger
- 1 tsp allspice
- Pinch of salt
- 200g black treacle
- 90g golden syrup
- 100g brown sugar
- 120g butter
- 1 large egg , lightly beaten
- 120ml milk

Preparation

1. Grease two 1-lb loaf tins. In bowl, add flour, oats, allspice, ground ginger, salt and baking powder. Mix.

2. In a pan over medium heat, add sugar, black treacle, golden syrup, butter. Heat until melted and remove from the heat. Let it cool for 5 minutes.

3. Pour butter/treacle mixture into flour and mix until combined. Add the egg and milk and stir until combined and smooth. Pour the batter evenly into the tins.

4. With no crisping plates installed, place the tins into Zone 1 and 2 drawers.

5. Select zone 1, select BAKE, set temperature to 140°C, and set time to 50 minutes. Select MATCH. Press the START/STOP button to begin cooking (use a skewer to check the cake. If it comes out clean, the cake is ready. If not, bake for a further 10 minutes covering with tin foil).

6. Let the cake cool then invert onto a plate. Cut into squares and serve.

… Afternoon Tea

Eggy Bread Sticks

Serves: 2 **Prep Time : 15 Mins** **Cook Time : 8 Mins**

Ingredients

- 6 white bread thick-cut slices
- 2 large eggs
- 120ml milk
- 1 tsp vanilla extract
- 1/2 tsp ground cinnamon
- Pinch of salt
- Icing sugar, for serving

Recipe tip:

- If possible, use slightly stale bread. It absorbs the egg mixture without becoming too soggy.
- Skip the sugar and cinnamon in the egg mixture and instead add a pinch of salt, black pepper, grated Parmesan and herbs like thyme or rosemary. Serve with a side of sausage for a savoury breakfast.

Preparation

1. Cut each slice of bread into 3 or 4 strips.

2. In a shallow dish, whisk together the eggs, sugar, milk, vanilla, cinnamon, and a pinch of salt until combined.

3. Dip each bread stick into the egg mixture. Allow any excess egg mixture to drip off.

4. With crisping plates installed, place the sticks into Zone 1 and 2 drawers.

5. Select zone 1, select MAX CRISP, and set time to 8 minutes. Select MATCH. Press the START/STOP button to begin cooking. When cooking time reaches 4 minutes, flip the sticks. Reinsert drawers to continue cooking.
Serve the eggy bread sticks warm with icing sugar, or your favourite fruits.

Afternoon Tea

Cheese Crackers

🔔 Serves: 4   🥣 Prep Time : 15 Mins   Cook Time : 8 Mins

Ingredients

- 220g plain flour
- 70 g grated mature Cheddar
- ½ tsp salt
- ½ tsp caster sugar
- 2 tsp baking powder
- 80g cold butter, cut into cubes
- 1 tbsp oil
- Cold water, as needed
- 2 tbsp melted butter, for brushing
- Optional toppings: dried herbs, sea salt flakes

Recipe tip:

- Mix minced garlic and a variety of fresh or dried herbs like basil, parsley, and thyme instead of Cheddar into the dough for Garlic Crackers.

Preparation

1. In a large bowl, add the flour, Cheddar, salt, and baking powder, mix until combined. Add the butter to the flour mixture. Using your fingers, mash the butter into flour until the mixture resembles breadcrumbs.

2. Add the oil, and add the water gradually, 1 tablespoon at a time, stirring with a fork, until the dough comes together and forms a ball.

3. Transfer the dough out onto a lightly floured surface and knead it gently a few times until smooth. Form into a ball and wrap in plastic wrap. Let rest for 10 minutes.

4. On a lightly floured surface, roll the dough into 1/2-cm thickness. Cut out small circles. Brick with a fork. With crisping plates installed, place the crackers into Zone 1 and 2 drawers.

5. Select zone 1, select BAKE, set temperature to 170°C, and set time to 8 minutes. Select MATCH. Press the START/STOP button to begin cooking. **Remove the crac**kers from the unit, brush with **melted butter an**d sprinkle with dried herbs or sea **salt flakes and le**t them cool completely on a wire **rack before serv**ing.

Afternoon Tea

Jam Stuffed Pie Pockets

Serves: 6   Prep Time : 15 Mins   Cook Time : 16 Mins

Ingredients

- 320g ready rolled shortcrust pastry
- Your favourite jam or Conserve
- 1 egg, whisked (for brushing)

For the Icing:
- 1/2 tsp vanilla extract
- 120g icing sugar
- 2 tbsp milk

Recipe Variation:

- **Bakewell Tart Inspired:** Fill the pie pockets with marzipan and raspberry jam. Sprinkle some flaked almonds on top before baking.
- **Mushroom and Stilton:** Sauté sliced mushrooms with garlic and thyme, then mix them with crumbled Stilton cheese for a rich and savoury filling.
- **Smoked Salmon and Cream Cheese:** Fill the pockets with smoked salmon slices and a layer of cream cheese.
- **Welsh Rarebit Style:** Spread a mixture of grated cheese, Worcestershire sauce, mustard, and a splash of milk on the dough rectangles before sealing.

Preparation

1. On a lightly floured surface, roll out the shortcrust pastry to about 1-cm thickness.

2. Cut out 6 rectangles from the dough. Place a tablespoon of jam in the center of each dough rectangles, leaving a small border around the edges. Fold the dough over the jam. Press the edges together using a fork to seal.

3. Brush the tops of the pie pockets with the egg.

4. With crisping plates installed, place the pie pockets into Zone 1 and 2 drawers.

5. Select zone 1, select BAKE, set temperature to 160°C, and set time to 16 minutes. Select MATCH. Press the START/STOP button to begin cooking. Flipping the pockets after 12 minutes. Remove from the unit and let cool.

6. In a bowl, whisk together the icing sugar, vanilla and milk until smooth. Once the pie pockets are cooled, drizzle the icing over the top of each pocket using a spoon. Serve.

Afternoon Tea

Irish Soda Bread

Serves: 4-6 **Prep Time : 20 Mins** **Cook Time : 35 mins**

Ingredients

- 480g plain flour
- 120g butter, softened
- 4 tbsp caster sugar
- 1 tsp bicarbonate of soda
- 1 tbsp baking powder
- 240ml buttermilk
- Pinch of salt
- 1 egg

For brushing:

- 60g butter, melted
- 40ml buttermilk

Preparation

1. In a small bowl, add 60g melted butter, 40ml buttermilk, mix and set aside.

2. In a large bowl, add flour, 120g butter, sugar, salt, bicarbonate of soda, baking powder. Mix until combined. Add the buttermilk, egg and knead until a dough is formed. Divide the dough into 2 equal balls.

3. Insert the crisper plates in Zone 1 and 2 drawers. Brush with oil. Place one loaf on each crisper plate. Using a sharp knife, slash the tops (X). Brush with butter/buttermilk mixture. Insert drawers in unit.

4. Select Zone 1, select BAKE, set temperature to 150°C and set time to 35 minutes. Select MATCH. Press START/STOP to begin.

5. When time reaches 10 minutes, remove drawers and brush each loaf with butter/buttermilk mixture. Reinsert drawers in unit to continue cooking.

6. When time reaches 30 minutes, remove drawers and flip each loaf. Reinsert drawers in unit to continue cooking.
When cooking is complete, remove from unit and let cool, then slice and serve.

INDEX

BREAKFAST

Carmalised Onion and Cheese Quiche 10
Sausage and Hash Brown Breakfast Casserole 12
Potato and Feta Frittata 13
Baked Sweet Potatoes 15
Jacket Potatoes 15
Chickpea Baked Eggs 16
Sausage and Egg Omelette 17
Corned Beef Hash 18
Corned Beef Fritters 19
Cheese and Onion Pasties 20
Baked Porridge Cups 21
Cheese on Toast 22
Broccoli and Mushroom Omelette........... 23
Celeriac Rosti 24

STARTERS & SIDES

Honey Roasted Parsnips 26
Breaded Baked Aubergine 27
Potato Gratin 28
Broccoli and Cauliflower Cheese 29
Courgette Pizza 30
Yorkshire Pudding 31
Cotswold dumplings 32
Salami and Cheese Loaded Chips 33
Sausage Rolls 34

DINNERS & SUPPERS

Sausage and Courgette Pasta Bake 36
Meatballs with Tomato Sauce 37
Rosemary Garlic Lamb Chops 38
Sausage and Peppers 39
Haggis Burger 40
Lamb Burgers 41
Popeseye Steak with Garlic Dill Butter ... 42
Barnsley Chops with Mint Sauce 43
Mustard Glazed Tomahawk Steak with Garlic and Parsley Sauce 44
Cheesesteak Sub Rolls 45
Stuffed Saddle of Lamb 46
Beef Bites and Gravy 47
Scotch Eggs 48
Shepherd's Pie 49
Mini Beef Wellingtons 50
Toad In The Hole 51
Forfar Bridie 52
Roasted Leg of Lamb and Potatoes 53
Minced Beef and Cheddar Casserole 54
Lemon Garlic Chicken and Orzo 55
Lemon Thyme Roast Chicken 56
Chicken Pasties 57
Sweet & Sticky Chicken Kebabs 58
Stuffed Chicken Breast 59
Glazed Chicken Thighs 60
Crispy Katsu Chicken 61
Rosemary Chicken with Roasted Vegetables 62
Crispy Chicken Breast Chunks 63
Salt and Pepper Chicken 64
Chicken Parmesan 65
Garlic Chicken Wings and Cheesy Pasta ... 66
Sweet and Spicy Chicken Wings 67
Baked Chicken And Gravy 68
Chicken Tikka Puff Pies 69

Butter Chicken 70
Chicken And Dumplings Casserole 71
Chicken Fajitas Bowls 72
Lemon and Butter Salmon 73
Kedgeree 74
Fish Fingers and Mushy Peas 75
Sweet Chilli Salmon with Egg Noodles 76
Salmon and Dill Parcels 78
Fish Cakes 80
Tuna Pasta Bake 81
Garlic Butter Prawns 82
Prawns and Broccoli with Herbed Rice 83
Breaded Cod Loins with Herb Butter
Potatoes 84

AFTERNOON TEA

Hot Cross Buns 86
Cheese Scones 87
Madeira Cake 88
Bakewell Tart 89
Apple Crumble Cake 91
Mini Victoria Sponge Cakes 92
Welsh Cakes 93
Custard Creams 94
Bara Brith 95
Sticky Toffee Pudding 96
Hobnob Biscuits 97
Ginger Biscuits 98
Carrot Cake Loaf 99
Chocolate Chip Butternut Squash Cake ... 100
Yorkshire Parkin 101
Eggy Bread Sticks 102

Cheese Crackers 103
Jam Stuffed Pie Pockets 104
Irish Soda Bread 105

Printed in Great Britain
by Amazon